T0135740

Autonomous Units as a Rule-based Concept for the Modeling of Autonomous and Cooperating Processes

von

Karsten Hölscher

Dissertation

zur Erlangung des Grades eines
Doktors der Ingenieurwissenschaften
– Dr.-Ing. –

Fachbereich Mathematik und Informatik
Universität Bremen

Tag des Promotionskolloquiums: 25. September 2008

Gutachter:
Prof. Dr. Hans-Jörg Kreowski
Prof. Dr. Martin Gogolla

Bibliografische Information der Deutschen Nationalbibliothek

Die Deutsche Nationalbibliothek verzeichnet diese Publikation in der Deutschen Nationalbibliografie; detaillierte bibliografische Daten sind im Internet über http://dnb.d-nb.de abrufbar.

©Copyright Logos Verlag Berlin GmbH 2008
Alle Rechte vorbehalten.

ISBN 978-3-8325-2090-8

Logos Verlag Berlin GmbH
Comeniushof, Gubener Str. 47,
10243 Berlin
Tel.: +49 030 42 85 10 90
Fax: +49 030 42 85 10 92
INTERNET: http://www.logos-verlag.de

Abstract

In this thesis autonomous units are presented as a concept to model autonomous processes. Autonomous units form a community with a common environment, in which they act and which they transform. They are based on rules, the applications of which yield changes in the environment. They are also equipped with an individual goal which they try to accomplish by applying their rules. A control condition enables autonomous units at any time and in any situation to select the rule that is actually applied from the set of all applicable rules. The formal semantics of a community as a whole and of each of its members is defined in two stages. In the sequential case only one unit can act at a time and the rule application of the involved units are interleaved with each other. In order to illustrate the sequential case, the formal concept of Petri nets is modeled by a community of autonomous units. Here every transition of the Petri net is realized as one autonomous unit. In the parallel case a number of actions take place in parallel at the same time. As an example, a colony of ants with a very simple foraging strategy is presented. In this case the parallel actions still occur in sequential order, so some preliminary ideas of a third stage are given. In this concurrent semantics, the autonomous units may act independently without chronological relations between them, unless a causal relationship demands a certain order of actions.

As further illustration, communities of autonomous units are applied to the domain of transport logistics. A transport network is modeled which consists of depots and their connections, unit loads, and trucks. The load units have to be transported from a source depot to a target depot by trucks. Here the trucks as well as the load units are modeled as autonomous units. How the unit loads will actually be transported by the trucks results from negotiations between all involved entities.

Two case studies that have actually been implemented using the graph transformation tool **GrGen** are presented in detail. The first case study deals with a model of the board game Ludo and the sequential process semantics of the corresponding community. Here every player as well as the die is modeled as an autonomous unit. It is shown how different strategies for the players can be specified.

The second case study deals with a model of a foraging ant colony and the parallel process semantics of the corresponding community. Here every ant is modeled as an autonomous unit. Foraging ants move in a random way, memorizing their path from the nest to the food source. On their way back they deposit pheromones on every part of their route. These pheromones then influence other foraging ants in the selection of their next step in a probabilistic way.

Some fundamental aspects of the semantics of rule-based systems in relation to the semantics of visual models are discussed, which form the conceptional background of this thesis.

Since control conditions are an essential part of the modeling with autonomous units, their efficient handling is the main challenge regarding the creation of a software tool. So some seemingly simple control conditions are investigated with respect to implementation.

Preface

Acknowledgements This thesis is based on research that has been carried out at the University of Bremen in the Research Group Theoretical Computer Science headed by Hans-Jörg Kreowski. I would like to thank him for giving me the opportunity to experience scientific research under his supervision and for providing me with good advice whenever I needed it. I also thank Martin Gogolla for introducing me to the UML and its shortcomings as well as enjoyable discussions and cooperation on formal modeling.

I am thankful to my former colleagues Peter Knirsch and Caroline von Totth for numerous scientific as well as not so scientific discussions. Peter also provided me with valuable information and suggestions on countless occasions. Sharing an office and thus most of the working time with him was very amusing. I am also deeply grateful to Renate Klempien-Hinrichs for her never-ending attendance, support and her motivating encouragement.

When I count my blessings, I count my loving wife Katrin at least twice and am grateful for her being the most important and supportive part of my life. I also thank my parents for their patience and support.

Finally, I gratefully appreciate the financial support which I have received for the work this thesis is based on from the DFG in the context of the project *UML-AID* and the *Collaborative Research Centre 637*.

Publications Parts of this thesis have already been published as conference papers or contributions to collections.

Chapter 3 subsumes the papers [HKK+07] and [HKK06b]. Chapter 4 elaborates on the results of [HKK06a]. Slightly adapted versions of the papers [HKL08], [KHK06], and [HKK08] constitute the Chapters 5, and 8, and 9 respectively.

Contents

Introduction

Today, most data processing systems comprise various interacting, possibly distributed, components. These components typically act autonomously but they may also communicate and interact with each other, spontaneously linking up to form a network. These components do not necessarily need to be stationary. Sometimes they even move or are carried around. Although the components act autonomously, their interaction and the system as a whole find the answer to a given problem.

In this thesis, autonomous units are suggested as a concept for modeling such systems. Autonomous units form a community with a common environment, in which they act and which they transform. Autonomous units are based on rules, the applications of which yield changes in the environment. They are also equipped with an individual goal which they try to accomplish by applying their rules. A control condition enables autonomous units at any time and in any situation to select the rule that is actually applied from the set of all applicable rules.

The motivation for the introduction of autonomous units as a modeling concept arises from the Collaborative Research Centre 637 *Autonomous Co-operating Logistic Processes* [FHS04]. This interdisciplinary collaboration focuses on the question whether and under which circumstances autonomous control may be more advantageous than classical control, especially regarding time, costs and robustness in logistics processes.

Logistics is a field characterized by mainly two types of dynamics. First, the organized supply with goods and information demands for controlled material and information flows. These flows are dynamic changes if seen from the operational point of view. To manage this kind of dynamics is the paramount challenge of logistics. Second, the whole setting is equipped with uncertainties and risks. Not all circumstances can be planned in advance; not all information needed is accessible, correct, or consistent at the point of scheduling. Occurring changes in the prerequisites can force the restart of the whole scheduling process repeatedly. Especially this type of dynamics is hard to cope with using the classical approaches. However, these difficulties exist in real world scenarios and being able to react to them can result in a great competitive advantage. The Collaborative Research Centre 637 tries to overcome these kinds of problems by avoiding a strictly centralized view and by passing control capabilities to the logistic objects in order to make them smarter.

The guiding principle of autonomous units is the possibility to integrate autonomous control into the model of the processes. This provides a framework for a semantically sound investigation of different mechanisms of autonomous control and their comparison. In more detail the aims are:

1. Algorithmic and particularly logistic processes shall be described in a very general and uniform way, based on a well-founded semantics.

2. The range of applications and included methods should comprise methods starting from classical process chain models like the one by Kuhn (see, e.g., [Kuh02]) or Scheer (see, e.g., [Sch02]) and the well-known Petri nets (see, e.g., [Rei98]) leading to agent systems (see, e.g., [Wei99]) and swarm intelligence (see, e.g., [KE01]).

3. The fact that autonomous units are based on rules provides the foundation for the dynamics of the processes. The process, transformation, and computation steps result from the application of rules, yielding local changes. Archetypes for this behavior are grammatical systems of all kinds (see, e.g., [RS97]) and term rewriting systems (see, e.g., [BN98]) as well as the domain of graph transformation (see, e.g., [Roz97, EEKR99, EKMR99]) and DNA computing (see, e.g., [PRS98]). The rule-based approach is meant to ensure the possibility of executing the semantics as well as to lay the foundation for formal verification.

4. The autonomous control should become apparent on two levels. On the one hand, a system comprises a community of autonomous units in an underlying environment. On this level, all the units are considered equal in the sense that they may act independently of other units (provided that the state of the environment is suitable for the application of the desired rules). Since no further control exists, the units act autonomously. On the other hand, transformation units as rule-based systems are typically nondeterministic, since at any time

several rules may be applicable, or the same rule may even be applicable at different positions. In this case, the autonomous control facilitates the selection of the different possibilities.

This thesis is structured as follows. In the next chapter, basic mathematical definitions and notations are presented together with a short tour of the formal groundwork of algebraic specification. Based on this, the abstract concept of a graph transformation approach is then introduced in Chapter 2, followed by the presentation of the concrete graph transformation approach that is used throughout this thesis. Communities of autonomous units are formally introduced in Chapter 3 and explained by means of two examples from the domain of swarm intelligence and Petri nets. In Chapter 4 and 5, two applications of autonomous units in the context of transport logistics are discussed. The first application focuses on a preliminary model of a transport net, in which trucks and packages plan their tours autonomously. Here, trucks and packages also negotiate the actual transportation in a very simple form. The second application is centered around a more sophisticated negotiation, which takes into account additional constraints, like e.g. arrival times. After that, two case studies are presented. In Chapter 6, a variant of the board game *Ludo* is modeled as a community of autonomous units. Here every player and the die are specified as autonomous units, with different strategies for the players. The model has been implemented in a prototypical way using a graph transformation engine, so some simulation results together with a rough summary of the technical details of the implementation are presented. In Chapter 7, a community of autonomous units is used to model an ant colony foraging for food. Here every ant is modeled as an autonomous unit with an individual memory. This case study has also been implemented, so a short discussion of the implementation and some simulation results follow. Chapter 8 focuses on the conceptional background of this thesis. Fundamental aspects of the semantics of rule-based systems are sketched and related to the semantics of visual models. Chapter 9 deals with considerations regarding the formal background of control conditions. It is investigated whether and under which circumstances the semantics of a control condition can be calculated and what restrictions the use of control conditions might impose on a potential implementation of autonomous units. The thesis closes with a summary and some concluding remarks.

Chapter 1

Foundations

1.1 Mathematical Notations and Definitions

The set of natural numbers $\{0, 1, 2, \ldots\}$ is denoted $\mathbb{N}$, $\mathbb{N} \setminus \{0\}$ is denoted $\mathbb{N}_+$, and the subset $\{0, 1, \ldots, n\}$ of $\mathbb{N}$ is denoted $[n]$.

Given a set A. Its powerset is denoted 2^A. A *string* over A is a word $a_1 a_2 \ldots a_n$ with $a_i \in A$ of length $n \geq 0$. A string with length 0 is called *empty string* and denoted λ. A^* denotes the set of all strings over A.

Given a mapping $f : A \to B$. The set A is called the *domain* of f, B is called the *codomain* of f, and $f(a), a \in A$ is called *image* of a. For a subset $C \subset A$ the restriction of f to C is denoted $f \mid C$ and is a mapping $f \mid C : C \to B$. It is defined as $(f \mid C)(x) = f(x)$ for all $x \in C$. Two mappings $f : A \to B$ and $g : A \to B$ are *equivalent*, denoted $f \equiv g$, if $f(x) = g(x)$ for every $x \in A$. $f(A)$ denotes the set of all images $\{f(a) \mid a \in A\}$, and is called *image* of A. Given the sets A, B, C and mappings $f : A \to B$ and $g : B \to C$. Then $(g \circ f)(x)$ denotes the concatenation $g(f(x))$ of g and f.

1.1 Definition (Families)
Given two sets I and M. A *family* in M indexed over I (or I-indexed family of M) is a mapping $f : I \to M$, denoted as $(m_i)_{i \in I}$, that assigns an element $m_i \in M$ to every $i \in I$. If M is the class of all sets, f defines a *family of sets*[1].

1.2 Definition (Finite and infinite sequence)
Let A be a set. An *infinite sequence* over A is a family over $\mathbb{N}$, denoted as

---

[1]In this case, f is not a true mapping, since a mapping is only defined on sets and not on classes. A formal definition is omitted here, since the intuition of a mapping suffices.

(a_i) or $(a_0, a_1, a_2, \ldots)$. If the domain of the mapping is $[n]$, the family is called *finite sequence* and denoted as $(a_i)_{i \in [n]}$ or $(a_0, a_1, \ldots, a_n)$.

If it is clear from the context whether or not a sequence is finite, both cases may be denoted (a_i), resp. $(a_0, a_1, a_2, \ldots)$. The set of all finite and infinite sequences over A is denoted as $Seq(A)$. A sequence is an ordered list, in which elements of the underlying set can appear multiple times at different positions.

The *length* of a sequence $a \in Seq(A)$ is the number of elements in the list and denoted $|a|$. It is $|(a_i)_{i \in [n]}| = n + 1$ and $|(a_i)| = \infty$. Please note that a binary tuple is a sequence of length 2.

A multiset is a generalization of a set, where each element of the set can have more than one membership.

1.3 Definition (Multiset)

A *multiset over A* is a tuple (A, m), where A is a set and $m : A \to \mathbb{N}$ is a mapping from A to the set of natural numbers. For $a \in A$, $m(a)$ is called the *multiplicity* of d. The *cardinality* of a multiset (A, m) is defined as $\sum_{a \in A} m(a)$ and denoted as $card((A, m))$. It is the total number of elements in a multiset including repeated memberships. If the cardinality of a multiset (A, m) is finite, (A, m) is called a *finite multiset*.

1.4 Definition (Set of all finite multisets)

Let A be a set. Then $A_* = \{(A, m) | card((A, m)) \in \mathbb{N}\}$ is called the *set of all finite multisets over A*.

The addition of two multisets $(A, m), (A, n) \in A_*$ can be defined by adding the multiplicities of the elements: $(A, m) + (A, n) = (A, k)$ with $k(a) = m(a) + n(a)$ for all $a \in A$. This addition operation is obviously commutative.

It is noteworthy that for every element $a \in A$, A_* contains a special multiset, in which the multiplicity of a is 1 and the multiplicity of all other elements of A is 0. More formally, for every $a \in A$ there is a multiset $(A, m) \in A_*$ such that $m(a) = 1$ and $m(a') = 0$ for $a' \in A, a' \neq a$. Such an element of A_* is called *singleton multiset*. A_*^1 denotes the set of all singleton multisets over A. Together with the addition operation defined above, every multiset originates from the commutative sum of its singleton multisets.

1.2   Short Introduction to Algebraic Specification

In order to use attributes for the graphs to be defined in the next chapter, some formal groundwork from algebraic specification is needed. For this reason, the needed concepts are briefly introduced and illustrated with a few examples. The following is taken from [EEPT06], for a deeper introduction see, e.g., [EM85].

1.5 Definition (Algebraic signature)
An *algebraic signature* (or just *signature*) $\Sigma = (S, OP)$ consists of a set S of sorts and a family of sets $OP = (OP_{w,s})_{w \in S^*, s \in S}$ of operation symbols. Operation symbols in $OP_{\lambda,s}$ are called *constant symbols*, while those operation symbols that are not constant symbols are called *operation symbols*.

Examples

- The signature NAT, intended to describe the natural numbers, has only one sort $S = \{Nat\}$, representing the numbers, and only one constant *zero*. It also comprises operation symbols for the successor, addition, and multiplication operations. It is

  - $OP_{\lambda,Nat} = \{zero\}$,
  - $OP_{Nat,Nat} = \{succ\}$,
  - $OP_{Nat\,Nat,Nat} = \{add, mult\}$.

  All the other sets are empty.

- The signature CHAR, intended to describe characters, also has only one sort $S = \{Char\}$, representing the characters, and only one constant a. Additionally, it comprises an operation *next* that implies an ordering on characters. It is

  - $OP_{\lambda,Char} = \{a\}$,
  - $OP_{Char,Char} = \{next\}$.

  All other sets are empty.

- The signature STRING uses the signature for characters. Thus, it has two sorts $S = \{Char, String\}$, and the two constants a and *String*. It also comprises operation symbols for the concatenation of two strings, for adding a character to a string, and for returning the first character of a string. It is

- $OP_{\lambda, Char} = \{a\}$,
- $OP_{\lambda, String} = \{String\}$,
- $OP_{Char, Char} = \{next\}$,
- $OP_{String String, String} = \{concat\}$,
- $OP_{Char String, String} = \{ladd\}$,
- $OP_{String, Char} = \{first\}$.

All other sets are empty.

A signature lays the formal foundation for the purely syntactical definition of terms. In order to provide a semantics for these syntactical constructs, an algebra is needed.

1.6 Definition (Σ-algebra)

Let $\Sigma = (S, OP)$ be a signature. A Σ-*algebra* $A = ((A_s)_{s \in S}, (op_A)_{op \in OP_A})$ then consists of

- an s-indexed family $(A_s)_{s \in S}$ of *carrier sets* for the sorts $s \in S$,

- *constants* $c_A \in A_s$ for every constant symbol $c \in OP_{\lambda, s}, s \in S$ and

- a family op_A of *operations* $op_A : A_{s_1} \dots \times A_{s_n} \to A_s$ for all $op \in OP_{s_1 \dots s_n, s}$; $s_i, s \in S$; $i = 1, \dots n$; $n \geq 1$.

Here $A_{s_1} \times A_{s_2} \dots \times A_{s_n}$ is the Cartesian product of the carrier sets where A_{s_i} belongs to the sort s_i. Operations are ordinary mappings, i.e. for all $a_i \in A_{s_i}$ $op_A(a_1, \dots, a_n) \in A_s$.

Examples

- A standard algebra A for the signature NAT from above is the following:

  - $A_{Nat} = \mathbb{N}$,
  - $zero_A = 0 \in A_{Nat}$,
  - $succ_A : A_{Nat} \to A_{Nat}$ with $x \mapsto x + 1$,
  - $add_A : A_{Nat} \times A_{Nat} \to A_{Nat}$ with $(x, y) \mapsto x + y$,
  - $mult_A : A_{Nat} \times A_{Nat} \to A_{Nat}$ with $(x, y) \mapsto x \cdot y$.

- The signature CHAR from above can be implemented by the following algebra C:

$$- C_{Char} = \{a, \dots, z, A, \dots, Z, 0, \dots, 9\},$$
$$- A_C = A \in C_{Char},$$
$$- next_C : C_{Char} \to C_{Char} \text{ with}$$
$$a \mapsto b, \dots, z \mapsto A, A \mapsto B, \dots, Z \mapsto 0, 0 \mapsto 1, \dots, 9 \mapsto a.$$

- A standard algebra D for the signature STRING from above specifies strings as words over characters and is defined on the character part like the algebra C. It is:

$$- D_{Char} = \{a, \dots, z, A, \dots, Z, 0, \dots, 9\},$$
$$- D_{String} = D_{Char}^*,$$
$$- a_D = A \in D_{Char},$$
$$- empty_D = \lambda \in D_{String},$$
$$- next_D : D_{Char} \to D_{Char} \text{ with}$$
$$a \mapsto b, \dots, z \mapsto A, A \mapsto B, \dots, Z \mapsto 0, 0 \mapsto 1, \dots, 9 \mapsto a.$$
$$- concat_D : D_{String} \times D_{String} \to D_{String} \text{ with } (s, t) \mapsto st,$$
$$- ladd_D : D_{Char} \times D_{String} \to D_{String} \text{ with } (x, s) \mapsto xs,$$
$$- first_D : D_{String} \to D_{Char} \text{ with}$$
$$\lambda \mapsto A, s \mapsto s_1 \text{ for } s = s_1 \dots s_n.$$

- Reconsider the signature NAT. Then the algebra A' with

$$- A'_{Nat} = \{0\},$$
$$- zero_{A'} = 0 \in A_{Nat},$$
$$- succ_A : A_{Nat} \to A_{Nat} \text{ with } x \mapsto 0,$$
$$- add_A : A_{Nat} \times A_{Nat} \to A_{Nat} \text{ with } (x, y) \mapsto 0,$$
$$- mult_A : A_{Nat} \times A_{Nat} \to A_{Nat} \text{ with } (x, y) \mapsto 0,$$

is also a valid, albeit degenerated, NAT-algebra.

1.7 Definition (Σ-homomorphism)

Let A and A' be Σ-algebras. Then a Σ-*homomorphism* $h : A \to A'$ from A to A' is a sort-indexed family of total mappings $h = (h_s : A_s \to A'_s)_{s \in S}$ such that

- $h_s(c_A) = c_{A'}$ for all $c \in OP_{\lambda,s}$, $s \in S$, and

- $h_s(op_A(a_1, \dots, a_n)) = op'_A(h_{s_1}(a_1), \dots, h_{s_n}(a_n))$
  for all $op \in OP_{s_1,\dots,s_n}, a_i \in A_{s_i}, i \in \{1, \dots, n\}$.

For every signature Σ a special algebra exists, which is used in the next chapter for the attributes of a type graph.

1.8 Definition (Final Σ-algebra)
Let $\Sigma = (S, OP)$ be a signature. Then the *final Σ-algebra* Z is defined by:

- $Z_s = \{s\}$ for each sort $s \in S$,

- $c_Z = s \in Z_s$ for each constant symbol $c \in OP_{\lambda,s}$,

- $op_Z : \{s_1\} \times \ldots \times s_n\} \to \{s\}$ with $(s_1 \ldots s_n) \mapsto s$ for each operation symbol $op \in OP_{s_1 \ldots s_n, s}$.

The fourth item in the algebra example list above is isomorphic to the final algebra for the signature Nat. Replacing 0 with *Nat* in A' yields the final algebra according to the definition.

Given a signature Σ, terms with and without variables can be constructed. These terms can be evaluated in every Σ-algebra.

1.9 Definition (Variables and terms)
Given a signature $\Sigma = (S, OP)$ and a family of sets $X = (X_s)_{s \in S}$ where each X_s is called the set of *variables* of the sort s. It is assumed that these X_s are pairwise disjoint and disjoint with OP. The family $T_\Sigma(X) = (T_{\Sigma,s}(X))_{s \in S}$ of *terms with variables* is inductively defined by:

- $x \in T_{\Sigma,s}(X)$ for all $x \in X_s$,

- $c \in T_{\Sigma,s}(X)$ for all constant symbols $c \in OP_{\lambda,s}$,

- $f(t_1, \ldots, t_n) \in T_{\Sigma,s}(X)$ for each operation symbol $f \in OP_{s_1 \ldots s_n, s}$ and all terms $t_i \in T_{\Sigma,s_i}(X), i \in \{1, \ldots, n\}$.

If the sets X_s are all empty, i.e. $X_s = \emptyset$ for all $s \in S$, the family of $T_\Sigma = (T_{\Sigma,s})_{s \in S}$ are called *terms without variables*. In this case it is $T_{\Sigma,s} = T_{\Sigma,s}(\emptyset)$.

1.10 Definition (Evaluation of terms without variables)
Given a signature $\Sigma = (S, OP)$ with variables X and a Σ-algebra A. The *evaluation* of the terms without variables $eval_A : T_\Sigma \to A$ with $eval_{A,s} = (eval_{A,s} : T_{\Sigma,s} \to A_s)_{s \in S}$ is defined by:

- $eval_{A,s}(c) = c_A$ for all constant symbols $c \in OP_{\lambda,s}$,

- $eval_{A,s}(f(t_1, \ldots, t_n)) = f_A(eval_{A,s_1}(t_1), \ldots, eval_{A,s_n}(t_n))$ for all terms $f(t_1, \ldots, t_n) \in T_{\Sigma,s}$ and operation symbols $f \in OP_{s_1 \ldots s_n, s}$.

For the evaluation of terms with variables, an assignment function which assigns values in the carrier sets to each variable is needed.

1.11 Definition (Assignment)

Given a signature $\Sigma = (S, OP)$ with variables X and a Σ-algebra A. An *assignment asg* $: X \to A$ is a family of assignment functions $asg_s : X_s \to A_s$ for all $s \in S$.

Now the evaluation of terms with variables can be defined using the assignment.

1.12 Definition (Evaluation of terms with variables)

Given a signature $\Sigma = (S, OP)$ with variables X, a Σ-algebra A, and an assignment $asg : X \to A$. Terms with variables are then evaluated by the *extended assignment* $\overline{asg} : T_\Sigma(X) \to A$ of the assignment asg, where $\overline{asg} = (\overline{asg}_s : T_{\Sigma,s}(X) \to A_s)_{s \in S}$ is defined by:

- $\overline{asg}_s(x) = asg_s(x)$ for all $x \in X_s$,

- $\overline{asg}_s(c) = c_A$ for all constant symbols $c \in OP_{\lambda,s}$,

- $\overline{asg}_s(f(t_1, \ldots, t_n)) = f_A(\overline{asg}_{s_1}(t_1), \ldots, \overline{asg}_{s_n}(t_n))$ for all terms $f(t_1, \ldots, t_n) \in T_{\Sigma,s}(X)$ and operation symbols $f \in OP_{s_1 \ldots s_n, s}$.

1.13 Definition (Term algebra)

The algebra $T_\Sigma(X) = ((T_{\Sigma,s}(X))_{s \in S}, (op_{T_\Sigma(X)})_{op \in OP})$ where the carrier sets consist of terms with variables and where the operations are defined by

- $c_{T_\Sigma(X)} = c \in T_{\Sigma,s}(X)$ for all constant symbols $c \in OP_{\lambda,s}$,

- $f_{T_\Sigma(X)} : T_{\Sigma,s_1}(X) \times \ldots \times T_{\Sigma,s_n}(X) \to T_{\Sigma,s}(X)$
  with $(t_1, \ldots, t_n) \mapsto f(t_1, \ldots, t_n)$ for all $f \in OP_{s_1 \ldots s_n, s}$.

is called the *term algebra* over Σ and X.

Chapter 2

Graph Transformation

This thesis deals with a formally well-founded modeling concept for autonomous interacting processes. It is typical for such processes that they exist in and change an environment that has a straightforward graphical representation. Whenever one has to do with such dynamic graph-like structures, graph transformation (see also [Roz97]) constitutes an adequate formal specification technique because it supports the visual and rule-based transformation of such structures in an intuitive and direct way. The ingredients of graph transformation are provided by a so-called graph transformation approach. In this chapter, the notion of a graph transformation approach as introduced in [KK99b] and slightly modified in [HKK06b] is recalled. It provides the foundation of the modeling of sequential processes. In order to allow for the modeling of parallel processes, the graph transformation approach is extended to a parallel graph transformation approach. Then the concrete graph model that is used throughout this thesis is introduced together with a compatible concrete graph transformation approach. The chapter closes with a short introduction to transformation units, which lay the foundation for autonomous units as introduced and discussed in the next chapter.

2.1 Graph Transformation Approaches

Two basic components of every graph transformation approach are a class of graphs and a class of rules that can be applied to these graphs. In many cases, rule application is highly nondeterministic — a property that is not always desirable. Hence, graph transformation approaches can also provide a class of control conditions so that the degree of nondeterminism of rule

application can be reduced. Moreover, graph class expressions can be used
in order to specify for example sets of initial and terminal graphs of graph
transformation processes.

2.1 Definition (Graph transformation approach)
Let ID denote an arbitrary but fixed set of identifiers. A *graph transformation approach* is a tuple $\mathcal{A} = (\mathcal{G}, \mathcal{R}, \mathcal{X}, \mathcal{C})$ where

- $\mathcal{G}$ is a class of *graphs*, called *environments*,

- $\mathcal{R}$ is a class of *graph transformation rules* such that every $r \in \mathcal{R}$ specifies a binary relation on graphs $SEM(r) \subseteq \mathcal{G} \times \mathcal{G}$,

- $\mathcal{X}$ is a class of *graph class expressions* such that each $x \in \mathcal{X}$ specifies a set of graphs $SEM(x) \subseteq \mathcal{G}$,

- $\mathcal{C}$ is a class of *control conditions* over ID, such that each $C \in \mathcal{C}$ specifies a set of sequences $SEM_{E,Change}(C) \subseteq Seq(\mathcal{G})$, where $Change \in \mathcal{G} \times \mathcal{G}$ and $E : ID \to 2^{\mathcal{G} \times \mathcal{G}}$. The *Change* relation defines arbitrary changes in the environment that may happen outside the control condition, while E assigns a binary relation on graphs as semantics for each identifier (also called identifier semantics). For this reason, control conditions have a loose semantics, which depends on the environment changes given by *Change* and the semantics of the identifiers. If environment changes are not considered, the semantics depends only on the identifier semantics, denoted as $SEM_E(C)$.

Please note that the overloaded SEM operator is used throughout this thesis for the semantics of different types of objects instead of using distinguished operators. This should not be a problem, since it is usually clear from the context to which type of parameter SEM is applied. The advantage of a more compact notion (contrary to a denotation with e.g. indices) yields the benefit of easier reading.

Given a set $P \subseteq \mathcal{R}$ of graph transformation rules, $SEM(P)$ is a shortcut notation for: $\bigcup_{p \in P} SEM(p)$.

The definition of a graph transformation approach serves as the foundation of a rule-based modeling concept for autonomous processes. In this definition, only one rule is applicable at a time. In order to obtain a suitable formal definition of parallel processes it is necessary to extend the assumptions on the given graph transformation approach, as introduced in [KK07]. For the parallel semantics definition situations are considered where a multiset of rules may be applied on the environment. This means that a number of different rules may be applied at once or even a single rule may be applied multiple times in one step.

2.2 Definition (Parallel graph transformation approach)
A *parallel graph transformation approach* is a tuple $\mathcal{A}_{||} = (\mathcal{G}, \mathcal{R}, \mathcal{X}, \mathcal{C})$ similarly defined as in the sequential case but with parallel rule application, i.e.:

- $\mathcal{R}$ is a class of *graph transformation rules* such that every $r \in \mathcal{R}_*$ specifies a binary relation on graphs $SEM(r) \subseteq \mathcal{G} \times \mathcal{G}$.

Since $\mathcal{R}$ is a set of rules, $r \in R_*$ comprises a selection of rules each with some multiplicity. Therefore, an application of r to a graph yielding a graph models the parallel and multiple application of several rules.

The multisets of rules in $\mathcal{R}_*$ are called *parallel rules*. A pair of graphs $(G, G') \in SEM(r)$ for some $r \in R_*$ is an application of the parallel rule r to G with the result G'. It may also be called a *direct parallel derivation* or a *parallel derivation step*.

2.2 Graphs

The graphs which are used throughout this thesis are attributed typed directed multigraphs. Such a graph consists of a set of typed nodes, a set of typed edges, and a source as well as a target mapping, which assign a source, resp. target node to every edge (thus allowing for multiple, equally directed edges of identical type between the same nodes). Additionally, every node and every edge is assigned a defined set of attributes according to its type.

An attributed typed directed multigraph corresponds to a typed attributed graph over an attributed type graph as presented in [EPT04] as a generalization of the concept of node attributed graphs introduced in [HKT02].

2.3 Definition (E-graph)
An *E-graph* is a tuple $G = (V_1, V_2, E_1, E_2, E_3, (src_i, tar_i)_{i=1,2,3})$ consisting of the sets

- V_1 and V_2, called *graph nodes* resp. *data nodes*,

- E_1, E_2, E_3, called *graph edges*, *node attribute edges*, and *edge attribute edges*, respectively, and source and target functions

- $src_1 : E_1 \rightarrow V_1$, $src_2 : E_2 \rightarrow V_1$, $src_3 : E_3 \rightarrow E_1$,

- $tar_1 : E_1 \rightarrow V_1$, $tar_2 : E_2 \rightarrow V_2$, $tar_3 : E_3 \rightarrow V_2$.

This notion distinguishes between two kinds of nodes and three kinds of edges, according to the different purposes they serve for the representation of attributed graphs.

An E-graph morphism is a structure preserving mapping of one E-graph to another one.

2.4 Definition (E-graph morphism)

Let G and H be E-graphs. An *E-graph morphism* M then is a tuple $M = (f_{V_1}, f_{V_2}, f_{E_1}, f_{E_2}, f_{E_3})$ where $f_{V_i} : G_{V_i} \rightarrow H_{V_i}$ and $f_{E_j} : G_{E_j} \rightarrow H_{E_j}$ for $i = 1, 2$; $j = 1, 2, 3$, such that:

- $f_{V_1}(src_{G,1}(e)) = src_{H,1}(f_{E_1}(e))$ for $e \in E_{G,1}$,

- $f_{V_1}(src_{G,2}(e)) = src_{H,2}(f_{E_2}(e))$ for $e \in E_{G,2}$,

- $f_{E_1}(src_{G,3}(e)) = src_{H,3}(f_{E_3}(e))$ for $e \in E_{G,3}$,

- $f_{V_1}(tar_{G,1}(e)) = tar_{H,1}(f_{E_1}(e))$ for $e \in E_{G,1}$,

- $f_{V_2}(tar_{G,2}(e)) = tar_{H,2}(f_{E_2}(e))$ for $e \in E_{G,2}$,

- $f_{V_2}(tar_{G,3}(e)) = tar_{H,3}(f_{E_3}(e))$ for $e \in E_{G,3}$.

An E-graph lays the foundation for attributed graphs, where nodes as well as edges can have arbitrarily many attributes.

2.5 Definition (Attributed graph)

Let $\Sigma = (S, OP)$ be a signature. An *attributed graph* $AG = (G, D)$ consists of an E-graph G together with a Σ-algebra D such that the disjoint union of the carrier sets equals the set of data nodes of G, i.e. $\biguplus_{s \in S} D_s = V_{G,2}$. For this reason there is an inclusion mapping $id_G, s : D_s \hookrightarrow V_{G,2}$ with $x \mapsto x$ for every $s \in S$.

An attributed graph morphism is a structure and attribute value preserving mapping of one attributed graph to another.

2.6 Definition (Attributed graph morphism)

Given a signature $\Sigma = (S, OP)$ and two Σ-algebras D_G and D_H. Let $AG = (G, D_G)$ and $AH = (H, D_H)$ be attributed graphs. Then an *attributed graph morphism* is a pair $f = (f_G, f_A)$ with an E-graph morphism $f_G : G \to H$ and a Σ-homomorphism $f_A : D_G \to D_H$, such that for all $s \in S$ it is $f_{A,s} \circ id_{H,s} = id_{G,s} \circ f_{G,V_2}$.

In order to define typed attributed graphs, a base graph which defines the actual typing is needed.

2.7 Definition (Attributed type graph)

An *attributed type graph* is an attributed graph $ATG = (TG, Z)$ where Z is the final Σ-algebra.

2.8 Definition (Typed attributed graph)

Let ATG be an attributed type graph. A *typed attributed graph* (AG, t) over ATG consists of an attributed graph AG together with with an attributed graph morphism $t : AG \to ATG$.

2.9 Definition (Typed attributed graph morphism)

Let (AG, t_G) and (AH, t_H) be typed attributed graphs. A *typed attributed graph morphism* is an attributed graph morphism $f : AG \to AH$ such that $t_H \circ f = t_G$.

Example Given the signatures STRING and NAT from page 7, the set of all data sorts used for attribution is $S_D = \{Char, String, Nat\}$. Figure 2.1 shows an attributed type graph $ATG = (TG, Z)$ for a basic student administration system. It is an attributed graph where each data node is depicted as a dotted circle and named after its corresponding sort, because the final Σ-algebra Z has sorts $Z_s = \{s\}$ for all $s \in S$. Solid rectangles denote graph nodes, solid arrows graph edges, dotted ellipses denote attribute nodes, and dotted edges denote node and edge attribute edges. The identifiers of the graph nodes are depicted inside the respective rectangles and those of the edges are depicted near the corresponding edge.

In this thesis type graphs are denoted in a more compact way, resembling UML class diagrams. Here graph nodes are depicted as rectangles comprising two compartments. The upper compartment contains the identifier of the graph element, while the lower one holds its attributes. The attributes are denoted line by line, each of which contains the identifier of the respective attribute edge and the attribute's sort, separated by a

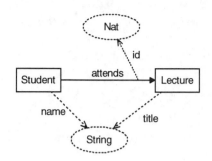

Figure 2.1: An attributed type graph

colon. Edges are denoted as arrows with a solid arrowhead, leading from the source graph node to the target graph node. They are labeled with a multiline text block, which contains the identifier of the graph edge in the first line and the attributes in a line wise manner analogously to the lower compartment of graph nodes. Figure 2.2 shows the graph from Figure 2.1 in this more compact notation.

Figure 2.2: Compact type graph notation

The type (name) of a node, resp. edge, is defined by the identifier of the corresponding node, resp. edge, in the type graph. Attribute names are likewise defined by the identifiers of the attribute edges in the type graph. Please note that the above definition of attributed typed graphs does not enforce the attribution of a graph node or graph edge, i.e. a concrete graph node may have fewer attributes than specified in the corresponding type graph. Also, since the node and edge attribute edges are defined as sets, attributes with the same name for nodes and edges of different types are not possible, i.e. it is not possible to have an attribute *id* for a node of type T_1 and for a node of type T_2. For the sake of clarity, identical attribute names may be used for different node or edge types in the following as a shortcut notation for e.g. names with indices. Throughout this thesis it is also assumed that every node and edge has exactly those attributes that are specified by the type graph. Since attributed typed directed multigraphs are the only graphs used throughout this thesis, they are hence simply

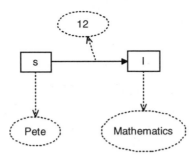

Figure 2.3: A sample attributed typed graph

called graphs and the corresponding mappings graph morphisms.

An attributed graph AG over ATG is depicted in Figure 2.3. Here only those algebra elements are shown explicitly that are actually used in the attribution of AG.

The graph AG is typed over ATG via the attributed graph morphism $t : AG \rightarrow ATG$ defined on nodes by $t(s) = Student$, $t(l) = Lecture$, $t(12) = Nat$, and $t(Pete) = t(Mathematics) = String$.

In this thesis, graphs are usually displayed in a way that resembles UML object diagrams. Nodes are depicted as rectangles with two compartments. In the upper compartment an optional identifier and the node type is notated, separated by a colon. In the lower compartment the attributes are depicted line by line, each of which contains the name of the attribute and its current value, separated by an equals sign. Attributes of type **String** are enclosed in double quotes. Edges are depicted as arrows, leading from the source node to the target node. A text block near the edge shows an optional identifier and its type, separated by a colon in the topmost line. Below that, the attributes are depicted analogously to the node attributes. If attributes are not shown or there are no attributes at all, a node may be depicted as a rectangle without the lower compartment or with an empty lower compartment. Figure 2.4 shows the compact notation of the graph from Figure 2.3 consisting of a node n1 of type **Student** with the attribute **name** and its value **Pete** and a node n2 of type **Lecture** with the attribute **title** and its value **Mathematics**.

Node n1 is connected to n2 by an edge of type **attends**, that has the attribute **id** with the value **12**. The identifier of this edge is omitted.

If node types have only one attribute or none at all, an even more compact notation can be used, replacing the rectangles with intuitive icons. Figure 2.5 shows the graph from Figure 2.4 in this even more compact no-

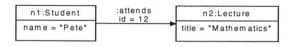

Figure 2.4: Compact graph notation

tation. Here the student node is depicted as a stick man and the lecture node as a book. The attribute value is then directly placed into the corresponding icon or near it, and so are optional identifiers. If there is only one type of edges, the edge type may be omitted and if they have only one attribute, only the attribute value may be depicted near the edge.

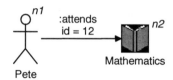

Figure 2.5: Alternative compact graph notation

2.3   An Approach to Graph Transformation

For the specifications in this thesis a graph transformation approach similar to the single-pushout approach (SPO) (cf., e.g., [EHK$^+$97]) is used for the definition of graph transformation rules and derivations. In order to formally define a rule, the concept of a subgraph is needed.

2.10 Definition (Subgraph)
Given two graphs $G = (V_{G,1}, V_2, E_{G,1}, E_{G,2}, E_{G,3}, (src_{G,i}, tar_{G,i})_{i=1,2,3}, D, t_G)$ and $H = (V_{H,1}, V_2, E_{H,1}, E_{H,2}, E_{H,3}, (src_{H,i}, tar_{H,i})_{i=1,2,3}, D, t_H)$ over the same type graph. H is a subgraph of G, denoted as $H \subseteq G$, if

- $V_{H,1} \subseteq V_1$,

- $E_{H,i} \subseteq E_i$, for $i \in \{1, 2, 3\}$,

- $src_{H,i} \equiv src_{G,i} \mid E_{H,i}, i \in \{1, 2, 3\}$,

- $tar_{H,i} \equiv tar_{G,i} \mid E_{H,i}, i \in \{1, 2, 3\}$.

Roughly speaking, a graph transformation rule consists of two graphs, the left-hand side L and the right-hand side R, such that a (possibly empty) subgraph $L \supseteq K \subseteq R$ exists. K is called the common part. A rule can be applied to a graph G, if a pattern as specified by L occurs as isomorphic copy in G, i.e. if a suitable attributed graph morphism $m : L \rightarrow G$ exists. Such a mapping is called a *match*. This mapping may not be unique, so that there may be several matches. The application of a rule then changes the part $m(L)$ of G in such a way that it becomes an isomorphic subgraph of R. This means that the corresponding elements of L that are not in K are deleted from $m(L)$, the elements of R that are not part of K are disjointly glued to $m(L)$ and the elements of $m(K)$ are preserved. The result of a rule application always has to be a graph, i.e. in case of a node deletion all adjacent edges of this node that are not part of $m(K)$ are also deleted. Since a match is not necessarily injective, it may map two different elements of L onto the same element of G. This leads to a conflict if one of the elements is in L but not in K while the other one is in K (i.e. one element is specified to be deleted, while the other one is specified to be preserved). The SPO approach deals with such conflicts by deleting the element in case of a conflicting definition.

Throughout this thesis, injective matches are usually used. Sometimes it may be necessary to allow the identification of certain graph elements in rules. In this case, those particular elements are marked in a special way, which will be explained where used.

2.11 Definition (Graph transformation rule)
Given a type graph ATG and a term algebra with variables $T_\Sigma(X)$. A *graph transformation rule* is a system $r = (L \supseteq K \subseteq R)$, where L, K and R are graphs which are typed over ATG and attributed over $T_\Sigma(X)$. The terms used in attributes of L and K may only be of the form $x \in T_{\Sigma,s}(X)$ for $x \in X$ or $c \in T_{\Sigma,s}(X)$ for all constant symbols $c \in OP_{\lambda,s}$.

Figure 2.6 shows a graph transformation rule with the name cashCheck, depicted in a rectangle labeled with the same name.

Its left-hand and right-hand sides are depicted in rectangles labeled L and R, respectively. Graph elements with identifiers are part of K, graph elements of L without identifiers are specified to be deleted, while graph elements of R without identifiers are specified to be added to the graph. In the given rule, a person, who is a customer with some id and who has an account with a saldo, cashes a check. The customer id, the saldo of the account and the amount of the check are each unknown in advance, so

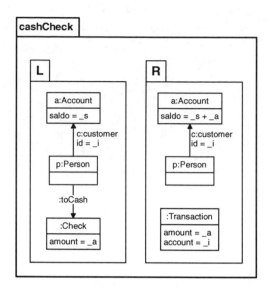

Figure 2.6: A sample graph transformation rule

variables are used as attribute values. A variable name is indicated in a
rule graph by an underscore in order to distinguish it from a constant.

For the formal definition of the application of a rule r, it is necessary
to define how to find an occurrence of the left-hand side of r in the graph.

2.12 Definition (Applicability of a rule)

Given a type graph ATG. Let G be a graph that is typed over ATG
and attributed over a Σ-algebra D. Let $r = (L \supseteq K \subseteq R)$ be a graph
transformation rule, where L is a graph typed over ATG and attributed
over $T_\Sigma(X)$ with the restrictions as defined above. A *match* is a typed
attributed graph morphism $m : L \to G$. The rule r is applicable on the
graph G if a match m exists.

Remember that the typed attributed graph morphism m comprises an
attributed graph morphism which in turn comprises a Σ-homomorphism
$m_{T_\Sigma(X)}$ and an E-graph homomorphism m_L. If the set of data nodes $V_{L,2}$
of L contains a variable $\_x$ of some sort $s \in S_D$, it is $m_{L,V_2}(\_x) = c$, where
$c \in V_{G,2}$ is a data node of the graph G. According to the definition of a
graph morphism, $m_{T_\Sigma(X),s}(\_x) = c$ also holds. In other words, variables
in attributes of the left-hand side match constant values in the graph. In
this way, the match determines the variable assignment needed for the
evaluation of potential terms in the application of a rule. More precisely, the

E-graph morphism together with the Σ-homomorphism defines mappings $asg_s : X_s \to D_s$ for all sorts $s \in S$ by $asg_s(x) = m_{T_\Sigma(X),s}(x)$ and thus an assignment $asg : X \to D$.

While it is obvious that the variables that occur in the left-hand side of a rule (i.e. which are actually attributes of nodes or edges) are assigned values from the graph, this is also the case for every variable in X. This is due to the fact that according to the definition of attributed graphs the whole set X of variables is part of the rule graphs as the set of data nodes. Since a match is a total mapping, it assigns arbitrary values to those variables that do not occur in the left-hand side.

In order to evaluate the terms in the right-hand side of a rule, an extended assignment $\overline{asg} : T_\Sigma(X) \to D$ with $\overline{asg} = (\overline{asg}_s : T_{\Sigma,s}(X) \to D_s)_{s \in S}$ is used. It is defined by

- $\overline{asg}_s(x) = asg_s(x)$ for all $x \in X$,

- $\overline{asg}_s(c) = c_D$ for all constant symbols $c \in OP_{\lambda,s}$,

- $\overline{asg}_s(f(t_1, \ldots, t_n)) = f_D(\overline{asg}_{s_1}(t_1), \ldots, \overline{asg}_{s_n}(t_n))$
  for all terms $f(t_1, \ldots, t_n) \in T_{\Sigma,s}(X)$ and operation symbols $f \in OP_{s_1 \ldots s_n, s}$.

The application of a rule deletes all adjacent edges of deleted nodes (and deleted edges) that are not part of the common part. Thus, the following notation is useful for the formal definition of a rule application. The edges in $F_i, i \in \{1,2,3\}$ that are adjacent to a graph node n are denoted as $E_{ad,i}(n) = \{e \in E_i \mid n = src_j(e) \text{ or } n = tar_j(e)\}$. For a subset N of the graph node set, the adjacent edges of the nodes in N are denoted $E_{ad,i}(N) = \bigcup_{n \in N} E_{ad,i}(n)$.

2.13 Definition (Rule application)

Let ATG be a type graph, $G = (V_1, V_2, E_1, E_2, E_3, (src_i, tar_i)_{i=1,2,3}, D, t_G)$ be an attributed graph that is typed over ATG and attributed over a Σ-algebra D, and a graph transformation rule $r = (L \supseteq K \subseteq R)$, where L, K, and R are graphs typed over ATG and attributed over $T_\Sigma(X)$ (with the restrictions as defined above for L and K). Let $m : L \to G$ be a match and $N_{del} = m_{V_1}(V_{L,1} \setminus V_{K,1})$ be the set of nodes to be deleted.

Then the application of the rule r on the graph G yields a new graph $G' = (V_1', V_2, E_1', E_2', E_3', (src_i', tar_i')_{i=1,2,3}, D, t_{G'} : G' \to ATG)$ defined by:

- $V_1' = V_1 \setminus N_{del} \uplus (V_{R,1} \setminus V_{K,1})$,

- $E_1' = E_1 \setminus m_{E_1}(E_{L,1} \setminus E_{K,1}) \setminus E_{ad,1}(N_{del}) \uplus (E_{R,1} \setminus E_{K,1})$,

- $E_2' = E_2 \setminus m_{E_2}(E_{L,2} \setminus E_{K,2}) \setminus E_{ad,2}(N_{del}) \uplus (E_{R,2} \setminus E_{K,2})$,

- $E_3' = E_3 \setminus m_{E_3}(E_{L,3} \setminus E_{K,3}) \setminus E_{ad,3}(N_{del}) \uplus (E_{R,3} \setminus E_{K,3})$,

- $src_1'(e) = \begin{cases} src_1(e) & \text{if } e \in E_1 \\ m_{V_1}(src_{R,1}(e)) & \text{if } e \notin E_1 \text{ and } src_{R,1}(e) \in V_{K,1} \\ src_{R,1}(e) & \text{otherwise} \end{cases}$

- $tar_1'(e) = \begin{cases} tar_1(e) & \text{if } e \in E_1 \\ m_{V_1}(tar_{R,1}(e)) & \text{if } e \notin E_1 \text{ and } tar_{R,1}(e) \in V_{K,1} \\ tar_{R,1}(e) & \text{otherwise} \end{cases}$

- $src_2'(e) = \begin{cases} src_2(e) & \text{if } e \in E_2 \\ m_{V_1}(src_{R,2}(e)) & \text{if } e \notin E_2 \text{ and } src_{R,2}(e) \in V_{K,1} \\ src_{R,2}(e) & \text{otherwise} \end{cases}$

- $tar_2'(e) = \begin{cases} tar_2(e) & \text{if } e \in E_2 \\ \overline{asg}(tar_{R,2}(e)) & \text{otherwise} \end{cases}$

- $src_3'(e) = \begin{cases} src_3(e) & \text{if } e \in E_3 \\ m_{E_1}(src_{R,3}(e)) & \text{if } e \notin E_3 \text{ and } src_{R,3}(e) \in E_{K,1} \\ src_{R,3}(e) & \text{otherwise} \end{cases}$

- $tar_3'(e) = \begin{cases} tar_3(e) & \text{if } e \in E_3 \\ \overline{asg}(tar_{R,3}(e)) & \text{otherwise} \end{cases}$

- $t_{G',V_1}(v) = \begin{cases} t_{G,V_1}(v) & \text{if } v \in V_1 \\ t_{R,V_1}(v) & \text{otherwise} \end{cases}$

- $t_{G',V_2} \equiv t_{G,V_2}$

- $t_{G',E_i}(e) = \begin{cases} t_{G,E_i}(e) & \text{if } e \in E_i \quad \text{for } i = 1,2,3 \\ t_{R,E_i}(e) & \text{otherwise} \quad \text{for } i = 1,2,3 \end{cases}$

- $t_{G',A_s} \equiv t_{G,A_s}$ for all $s \in S$.

Such a rule application is also called *direct derivation*.

Applying the rule from Figure 2.6 leads to the deletion of the check and its adjacent edges. The saldo of the person's account is recalculated. The new value is the sum of the previous saldo and the amount of the check.

Additionally, a node of type **Transaction** is added, which stores the amount as well as the customer id. The left part part of Figure 2.7 shows a graph with a customer named **Ada**, who has an account with the saldo 1000 and the customer id 1465. She cashes a check with the amount 100. The right part of the Figure shows the graph after applying the rule **cashCheck**.

The **Check** node has been deleted, the saldo of Ada's account has been adjusted, and a **Transaction** node for later reference has been added.

As we have seen, the left-hand side specifies a situation that has to be present in the graph for a rule to be applicable. But sometimes it is also useful to be able to specify a situation that is not wanted in the graph for a rule to be applicable. Consider the check cashing situation introduced earlier with additional information about the issuer of the check, who in this case happens to be another customer of the same financial institution. This can be represented in the graph by an **issuer** edge leading to the **Check** node from a respective **Person** node, which in turn is connected via a **customer** edge to an **Account** node. If customers of the financial institution have no money left in their accounts, they are flagged with a loop edge of type **broke**. Obviously, a check that has been issued by a broke customer must not be cashed. This can be realized by a negative application condition (NAC), as depicted in Figure 2.8. A NAC of a rule $(L \supseteq K \subseteq R)$ is a graph N with $L \subseteq N$. The rule is not applicable on a graph G if the match $m : L \to G$ can be extended to $q : N \to G$ such that $m \equiv q \mid L$. If no such q can be found, the match m *satisfies* the NAC and the rule is applicable.

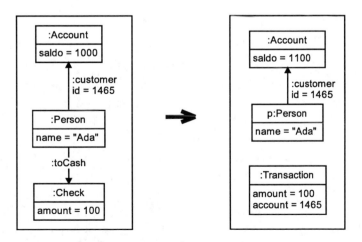

Figure 2.7: Sample graph before and after rule application

A graph transformation rule can have several negative application conditions. In this case the rule can only be applied if a match exists that satisfies every NAC. In the example from Figure 2.8 the rule cannot be applied if the customer who issued the check is flagged as **broke**. Please note that attribute values which are not needed in the course of a rule application are not denoted in the rule figures. This means that an existing attribute value of a node or edge remains unchanged by the application of the rule. The same is true if attributes that are depicted in the left-hand side of a rule do not occur in its right-hand side.

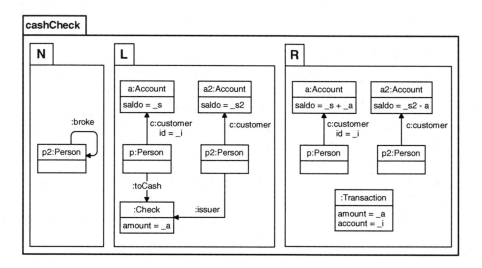

Figure 2.8: A sample rule with a negative application condition

Sometimes it is necessary to specify additional constraints in the left-hand side of a rule. This can be done by a Boolean expression which has to be evaluated according to the match. This expression is part of the left-hand side and called *application condition* (AC). In the previous example, an NAC has been used in order to prohibit the cashing of a check issued by a fund-less customer. This can also be realized by an application condition as can be seen in Figure 2.9. Here the AC, which is depicted in the rectangle in the lower left of L, states that the saldo of the issuer's account must be greater or equal to the amount of the check. The variables that are used in the AC are determined by the respective match. Thus the AC is evaluated for a given match, and only if it evaluates to **true**, the rule may be applied. Negative application conditions may also have an AC, meaning

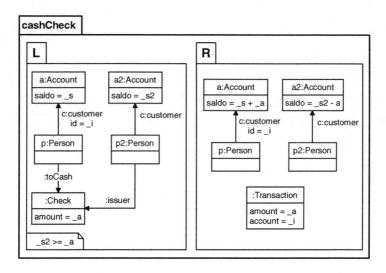

Figure 2.9: A sample rule with an application condition

that a match does not satisfy the NAC if there is a mapping q as defined above **and** the AC of the NAC evaluates to **true** according to the extended match q.

It is also possible to specify further constraints for the rule application by using a post condition. A post condition is part of the right-hand side of a rule and is a Boolean expression. It is evaluated after a virtual rule application using the variable bindings determined by the respective match. If it evaluates to **false** the rule cannot be applied. The previous example can also be realized by a post condition as depicted in Figure 2.10. There is no NAC and no AC, but a post condition as part of the right-hand side specifying that after the application of the rule the saldo of the issuer's account has to be greater or equal to null. The post condition is denoted in the lower left of **R**. The effect of the three variants above is equivalent. Whenever the amount of the check exceeds the issuer's saldo, the rule that implements the cashing of the check must not be applied (provided that the **broke** flag has been set correctly in advance in the first variant).

In the course of this thesis, graph transformation rules may have parameters, denoted in brackets behind the rule name. This is no formal feature, but simply a shortcut notation for a set of rules which differ only in specific parts. Rule parameters can be nodes and edges and the identifiers of the parameters have to be used in the left-hand side of the rule. The concrete rule can be obtained by a substitution of the parameters with the actual

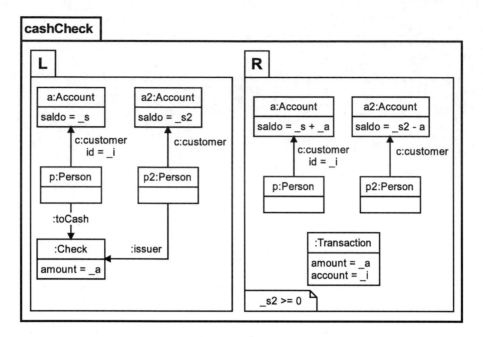

Figure 2.10: A sample rule with a post condition

nodes and edges.

In the following, a suitable signature Σ_{GT} together with the corresponding final algebra Z_{GT} and a Σ_{GT}-algebra D_{GT} is assumed without providing formal definitions. This signature contains sorts representing strings over characters (including special characters), Booleans and integers. It also comprises the usual operation symbols for these sorts, like string concatenation, equality tests, integer arithmetic, and so on. The algebra defines the expected carrier sets and operations. Since we also need terms and variables later on, T_{GT} hence denotes the corresponding term algebra over Σ_{GT} and a suitable set of variables X, the names of which starting with an underscore.

2.4   Graph Transformation Units

This thesis focuses on the concept of autonomous units, which are a generalization of graph transformation units. For this reason, a short introduction to transformation units is provided in the following. Graph transformation units, introduced in [KK99b, KK99a, Kus00b], are an approach-independent concept for programming by applying rules and imported transformation units to graphs, starting in an initial and ending in a terminal graph. This transformation process has to obey a so-called control condition, i.e. the device to select how rules or imported transformation units are to be combined in the transformation process executed by the unit.

2.14 Definition (Graph transformation unit)

Let $\mathcal{A} = (\mathcal{G}, \mathcal{R}, \mathcal{X}, \mathcal{C})$ be a graph transformation approach. Then a *transformation unit over* $\mathcal{A}$ is a system $tu = (I, U, R, C, T)$ where

- $I, T \in \mathcal{X}$ are graph class expressions,

- $U \subseteq ID$ is a finite set of identifiers,

- $R \subseteq \mathcal{R}$ is a finite set of rules, and

- $C \in \mathcal{C}$ is a control condition.

The graph class expressions I and T denote classes of initial and terminal graphs, respectively. Initial graphs define valid input for a transformation unit and terminal graphs specify what kind of graphs are expected as a result of its computation.

U defines the import of a transformation unit, thus it contains the identifiers of transformation units to import. If $U = \emptyset$ then no other transformation units are imported, meaning that we have an unstructured transformation unit of the lowest level. In the following, it suffices to consider a hierarchical import structure, i.e. each transformation unit may only import transformation units of a lower level. This facilitates the definition of the semantics given below. For transformation units that may have a cyclic import structure, a fix-point semantics is developed in [KKS97].

Transformation units have an operational semantics that is defined as a binary relation on graphs. The intuition is that an initial graph is transformed into a terminal graph by stepwise execution of some sequence over the imported transformation units and the rules, where a step for $t \in U$ consists of using an adequate pair in the semantics of t and a step for $r \in R$ consists of applying r, such that the control condition – usually restricting the set of allowed sequences – is obeyed.

Let $tu = (I, U, R, C, T)$ be a transformation unit and E_{tu} an identifier mapping that assigns the rule application $SEM(r)$ to the identifier of each $r \in R$ and the semantics $SEM(t)$ to the identifier of each $t \in U$. Then $(G, H) \in SEM(tu)$ if

- $G \in SEM(I)$,

- $H \in SEM(T)$,

- there is a finite sequence $(G_i)_{i \in [n]} \in Seq(\mathcal{G})$ such that $G_0 = G, G_n = H$ and, for $i = 1, \ldots, n$, either $(G_{i-1}, G_i) \in SEM(t)$ for some $t \in U$ or $(G_{i-1}, G_i) \in SEM(r)$ for some $r \in R$, and

- $(G_i)_{i \in [n]} \in SEM_{E_{tu}}(C)$, which means that the sequence $(G_i)_{i \in [n]}$ must be allowed by the control condition C and the specific identifier semantics E_{tu}.

Chapter 3

Autonomous Units

In this chapter, the basic concept of autonomous units as a modeling approach for data processing systems with autonomous components is introduced. The semantics of a community of autonomous units is then defined in three stages. First of all a simple sequential semantics is introduced. This semantics is merely suitable for systems that allow only one action at a time. This covers not only most algorithms and sequential processes, but also card and board games. On the second stage a parallel semantics is defined. Here a number of actions take place in parallel at the same time. This allows for an adequate description of parallel derivations in L systems and some graph transformation approaches, the firing of Petri nets, and parallel algorithms and processes. While the parallel actions in this semantics occur in sequential order, the third stage defines a concurrent semantics with no chronological relations between the acting units. Here the autonomous units may act independently, unless a causal relationship demands a certain order of actions.

Autonomous units are illustrated employing two examples. On the one hand place-transition systems are modeled as autonomous units. Here every transition can be considered as one unit. On the other hand an ant colony's food transport is described as a system of autonomous units. Here every ant is modeled as an autonomous unit.

The author of this thesis had a significant part in the development of the new concept of autonomous units, which is a contribution of the Research Group Theoretical Computer Science headed by Prof. Dr. Hans-Jörg Kreowski at the University of Bremen to the Collaborative Research Centre 637 *Autonomous Cooperating Logistic Processes* [FHS04].

3.1   Communities of Autonomous Units

Autonomous units form a community with a common environment, which they may transform. For the sake of simplicity we represent the environments as graphs. But graphs are used in a quite generic sense, including all sorts of diagrams. They may be directed, undirected, labeled or attributed. Since graphs may comprise different subgraphs and different connected components it is also possible to use sets, multisets, and lists of graphs as well as arbitrarily structured graphs as environments.

An autonomous unit is based on a graph transformation approach from Definition 2.1 and consists of a set of graph transformation rules, a control condition, and a goal. Moreover, it can import other units to which it may delegate auxiliary tasks. In this first approach, which has been introduced in [HKK$^+$07], the import feature is not considered further. For an introduction of autonomous units with import see [HKK06b, KK07]. The graph transformation rules contained in an autonomous unit *aut* define all transformations this unit can perform. The control condition regulates the application process. For example, it may require that rules are applied in a given sequence or that a sequence of rules is applied as long as possible. The goal of a unit is a graph class expression specifying what the transformed environment should look like.

3.1 Definition (Autonomous unit)
An *autonomous unit* is a system $aut = (g, P, c)$ where $g \in \mathcal{X}$ is the *goal*, $P \subseteq \mathcal{R}$ is a set of graph transformation rules, and $c \in \mathcal{C}$ is a control condition. The components of *aut* are also denoted by g_{aut}, P_{aut}, and c_{aut}, respectively.

Autonomous units are intended to act or interact within a community in order to modify the common environment. In the sequential case, these modifications take place in an interleaving manner. A community of autonomous units comprises an overall goal that should be achieved, an environment specification that specifies the set of initial environments the community may start working with, and a set of autonomous units.

3.2 Definition (Community)
A triple $COM = (Goal, Init, Aut)$ is called a *community*, where $Goal, Init \in \mathcal{X}$ are graph class expressions called the *overall goal* and the *initial environment specification*, respectively, and Aut is the set of the participating autonomous units.

Example Place/Transition Systems

Place/Transition (P/T) systems are a frequently used kind of Petri nets that can be modeled as a system of autonomous units. The P/T net with its marking is regarded as the environment. Transitions are modeled as rules. The firing of a transition defines a rule application that changes the marking in the usual way. Class expressions may be single markings, which define themselves as semantics. A further class expression *all* is also needed, meaning that all environments are permitted. The control condition consists solely of the standard condition *free*, which defines all pairs of environments and imposes no restrictions on the application of rules.

Let a transition t be an autonomous unit $aut(t) = (all, \{t\}, free)$. Then a P/T net with the set of transitions T and initial marking m_0 is modeled as a community of autonomous units $COM(N, m_0) = (all, m_0, \{aut(t) \mid t \in T\})$.

Example Ant Colony

For further illustration, a simplified example from the domain of swarm intelligence is sketched.

Consider an ant colony consisting of an arbitrary number of ants. The ants leave their home, the anthill (or nest), and search for food. Once an ant discovers a food source, it takes some of the food and carries it back to the nest. Then it takes off to fetch more food. Such a scenario can be modeled by graph transformation employing the type graph depicted in Figure 3.1.

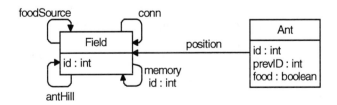

Figure 3.1: The type graph for the ant colony model

Ants are represented by nodes of type **Ant**. In order to distinguish the different ants, every **Ant** node has an attribute **id** with a unique value. Whether or not an ant carries food is indicated by the attribute **food**. Ants can be located at fields, represented by nodes of type **Field**. A **Field** node has an attribute **id** which carries a unique field identifier. This attribute value is used to prohibit an ant from directly walking back to a previously visited field. Thus the ant has to memorize this field. The memorization is modeled by the attribute **prevID**, which stores the identifier of the previously visited field. The anthill and the food source are modeled as special fields, i.e. the field representing the nest has a loop edge of type **antHill**, and the field representing the food source has a **foodSource** loop edge. Fields are interconnected by edges of type **conn**, indicating that an ant can move along this edge from one field to another one. The actual position of an ant is indicated by an edge of type **position**, which connects the **Ant** node with the corresponding **Field** node. In order to find their way back to the nest, ants memorize their individual path to the food source by edges of type **memory**. These edges have an attribute **id**, which carries the same value as the corresponding **id** attribute of the **Ant** node.

In this example, the initial environment graph depicted in Figure 3.2 consists of a fixed number of **Field** nodes, two of which are marked with an **antHill**, resp. a **foodSource** loop edge. The fields are connected by **conn** edges in a bidirectional way, i.e. every **conn** edge leading from one field to another is duplicated to yield a connection in the opposite direction. In the picture the **conn** type names are left out for the sake of compactness. The fields are connected in such a way that they form a grid. Additionally, diagonal connections, which obviously form the shortest path, connect the anthill with the food source. Every ant is represented by its own **Ant** node, each of which carries a unique identifier in the **id** attribute. Initially, every **Ant** node is connected to the field marked as anthill by an edge of type **position**, and its **food** value is set to false. Figure 3.2 shows a sample initial environment graph with a anthill, a food source, fourteen fields and three ants.

If an ant does not carry any food, it moves to a random but adjacent field, unless it has visited that field in the previous step. Figure 3.3 shows the according graph transformation rule.

As explained earlier, the parameter of the rule is a placeholder for the actual ant node. The left-hand side of the rule detects a situation where the ant **a** is positioned on one field and carries no food. An adjacent field is determined, which has to be different from the field that has been visited by the ant in the previous step, as enforced by the application condition in the lower left. The negative application condition **N1** ensures that the adjacent field is not the food source, because a specific rule deals with the situation where the ant is positioned directly next to the food source. The negative

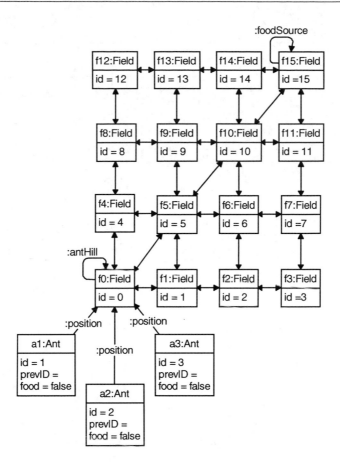

Figure 3.2: The initial environment of the ant colony model

application condition **N2** ensures that the adjacent field is not the anthill either, since it makes no sense for an ant to walk back to the anthill without carrying any food. The application of this rule yields the replacement of the **position** edge, simulating a step of the ant from the first field to the adjacent field. Since the ant does not carry any food, it also memorizes this step by inserting a **memory** edge with the **id** attribute value matching the **id** attribute value of the ant. Additionally, the **prevID** attribute of the ant is updated by storing the **id** of the originally visited field **f1**.

On reaching a field that is adjacent to the food source, the rule **walkTo-Food**, as depicted in Figure 3.4, can be applied.

Its left-hand side detects the situation where the ant (which is again

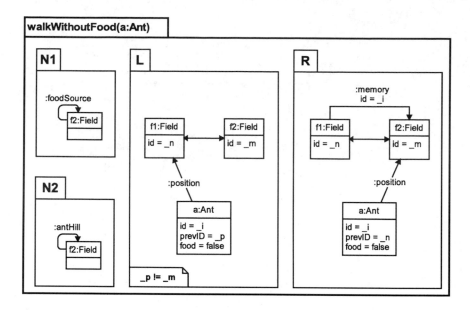

Figure 3.3: The rule walkWithoutFood of an ant

represented by the parameter a:Ant), which carries no food, is positioned
on a field that is directly connected to the food source. In this case, it is
not necessary to consider the previously visited field, since the ant should
not have been at the food source yet. If the rule is applied, the ant is
positioned on the field representing the food source. A memory edge is
inserted analogously to the rule walkWithoutFood. Additionally, the ant
picks up some food, which is indicated by setting the food attribute value
to true. The attribute value prevID is not considered for an ant carrying
food, so it is left unchanged.

Now the ant is carrying food and retraces its memorized path back to
the anthill. The corresponding rule is depicted in Figure 3.5. It detects the
memorized step by the memory edge leading from another field f2 to the
field f1 on which the ant is currently located. Of course this memory edge
needs to have the same id as the ant and the ant's food attribute value has
to be true. The negative application condition ensures that the field f2 is
not the anthill, because this situation is handled by a different rule.

If this rule is applied, the ant takes a step from field f1 to field f2
by inserting a correspondingly connected position edge and deleting the
original one. Additionally, the memory edge is deleted, since it is not needed
anymore.

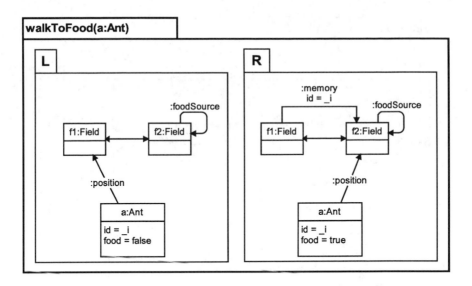

Figure 3.4: The rule walkToFood of an ant

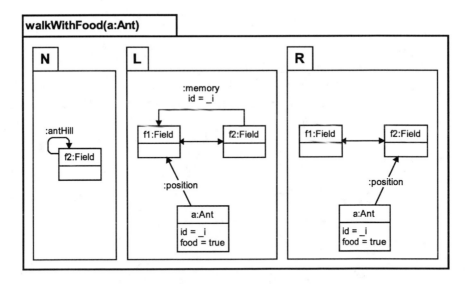

Figure 3.5: The rule walkWithFood of an ant

If the ant reaches the field that it visited as the first step on the way to the food source, the rule depicted in Figure 3.6 is applicable. It detects the aforementioned situation. The application of this rule simulates the

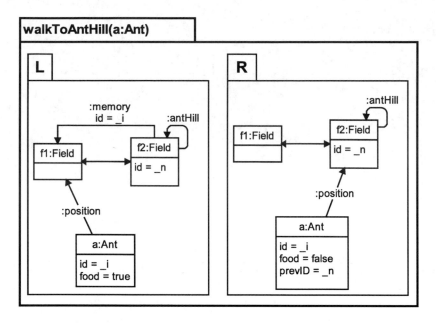

Figure 3.6: The rule walkToAntHill of an ant

ant moving back to the anthill, dropping the food, and preparing to leave
for food again. This is technically achieved by inserting a corresponding
position edge and deleting the original one. Additionally, the food attribute
of the ant is set to false and the prevID field is set to the id of the anthill.

In this model, every ant is represented by an autonomous unit as depicted in Figure 3.7.

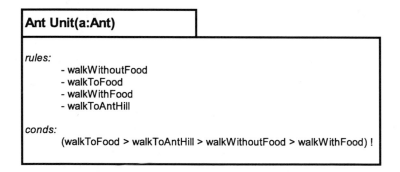

Figure 3.7: The autonomous unit Ant Unit

The ant units manifest themselves in the environment through the corresponding **Ant** nodes. For this reason, the autonomous unit **Ant Unit** has a formal parameter **a:Ant**. Analogously to the parameters of rules, parameters of autonomous units are not a formal feature, but a shortcut notation abstracting from the actual units. Imagine e.g. two **Ant Units**, manifested in the environment by corresponding **Ant** nodes with the **id** attribute values 1 and 2, respectively. Then the **Ant Unit** with the **id** value 1 contains the graph transformation rules in which the actual **Ant** nodes have the **id** attribute value 1. Analogously, the other **Ant Unit** contains the graph transformation rules in which the **Ant** nodes have **id** attribute value 2. As an abstraction mechanism for these actual rules and nodes, parameters for the autonomous units are used, which are directly employed in the corresponding rules.

The **Ant Unit** has no explicit goal, which means that it allows every environment as a goal. The rules that have been introduced earlier are all part of an **Ant Unit**, but they may not be applied freely. The control condition imposes the following restriction on the rule application process. First of all, the subcondition in brackets is applied as long as possible. This subcondition yields a single rule application by specifying different priorities for the contained rules, as indicated by the operator '>'. Only one of the four rules is allowed to be applied in every derivation step, depending on their priorities. If the leftmost rule is applicable, then it has to be applied, completing the subcondition. Only if it is not applicable, the rules denoted further to the right may be applied. This means that the application of the rule **walkWithFood** is only allowed by the subcondition if all of the other three rules are not applicable. Please note that in this case the rules are specified in such a way that only one of them is applicable at any given time. Should none of the four rules be applicable, the whole control condition is completed. This can never happen in a suitable environment, since an ant can always walk.

A collection of foraging ants is then modeled as a community of **Ant Units**. This community has no explicit overall goal, i.e. it allows every environment as a goal. The initial environment has to contain a number of **Field** nodes. Every **Field** node has to be connected to at least two other **Field** nodes by edges of type **conn** in both directions. Exactly one field has to have a loop edge of type **antHill**, and exactly one other field a loop edge of type **foodSource**. For every **Ant Unit** of the community there also has to be an **Ant** node with a unique **id** attribute value, connected to the **Field** marked as anthill by a **position** edge. The **food** attribute value of every ant has to be **false**.

In the following sections the semantics of communities of autonomous units is defined in three variants. The most simple one is the sequential semantics, which is merely suitable for systems that allow only one action at a time. The parallel semantics allows for activities to take place in parallel. The third variant covers true concurrency. Only causally related activities (e.g. one action needs something that is created by another action) occur in chronological order. Other activities may happen at any time.

3.2   Sequential Semantics

An autonomous unit works on and modifies an underlying environment, trying to achieve its goal. Its semantics is defined as a set of transformation processes being finite or infinite sequences of environment transformations. Each such transformation is either the application of a local rule or an environment change. Such a change is typically performed by another autonomous unit that is working on the same environment. Let $\mathcal{G}$ be the class of environment graphs, then these changes are defined as a binary relation $Change \subseteq \mathcal{G} \times \mathcal{G}$ of environments. Autonomous units act in an autonomous way by choosing only those rules that are allowed by its control condition in every step.

3.3 Definition (Sequential *aut*-process)
Let $aut = (g, P, c)$ be an autonomous unit and $Change \subseteq \mathcal{G} \times \mathcal{G}$. A *sequential process of an autonomous unit* with respect to *Change* is an infinite graph sequence $s = (G_i) \in Seq(\mathcal{G})$ or a finite graph sequence $s = (G_i)_{i \in [n]} \in Seq(\mathcal{G})$ such that for $i \in \mathbb{N}_+$ if s is infinite and for $i \in \{1, \ldots, |s|\}$ if s is finite

- $(G_{i-1}, G_i) \in SEM(r)$ for some $r \in P$ or $(G_{i-1}, G_i) \in Change$, and

- $s \in SEM_{Change}(c)$.

The set of all sequential *aut*-processes with respect to *Change* is denoted $SEQ_{Change}(aut)$.

Assuming that the community is closed, i.e. everything that happens is caused by its members, the changes of the environment that occur besides the changes of a particular participating unit must be activities of the other units in the community. This is reflected in the following definition.

3.4 Definition (Change relation)

Let $COM = (Goal, Init, Aut)$ be a community of autonomous units. Then the *change relation* with respect to aut is given for each $aut \in Aut$ by those rules that are composed of rules of the autonomous units in COM without aut, i.e.

$$Change(aut) = \bigcup_{a \in Aut - \{aut\}} SEM(P_a).$$

Since the application of rules allows direct derivations, a first simple semantics for communities of autonomous units is obtained by sequential composition. This includes finite as well as infinite processes. The sequential processes have to start in an initial environment.

3.5 Definition (Sequential process)

Let $COM = (Goal, Init, Aut)$ be a community of autonomous units. A *sequential process* is then defined as a finite (also called *computation*) or infinite graph sequence $s = (G_i) \in Seq(\mathcal{G})$ such that $s \in SEQ_{Change(aut)}(aut)$ for all $aut \in Aut$.

In this sense a sequential process is an arbitrary sequential composition of rule applications by autonomous units, obeying the control condition of all involved units. The set of all sequential processes is denoted as $SEQ(Aut)$. Accordingly, $SEQ(Init, Aut)$ contains all processes which start in an initial environment, and $SEQ(Goal, Init, Aut) = SEQ(COM)$ contains all finite sequential processes which additionally terminate in an environment that meets the goal.

In the latter case the semantics can also be defined by an input-output relation $REL_{SEQ}(COM)$. This describes the computation without intermediate steps: it is $(G, H) \in REL_{SEQ}(COM)$ if $(G_i)_{i \in [n]} \in SEQ(COM)$ exists such that $G = G_0$ and $H = G_n$. Even for arbitrary processes the goal specification makes sense, since it can be determined whether $Goal$ has been reached for processes (G_i) in intermediate steps: $G_{i_0} \in SEM(Goal)$ for some $i_0 \in \mathbb{N}$?

The sequential processes $SEQ(Aut)$ of a set Aut of autonomous units and the sequential processes of one of its members are strongly connected:

$$SEQ(Aut) = SEQ_{SEQ(Aut - \{aut\})}(aut).$$

So every sequential process is an *aut*-process for every autonomous unit in Aut and vice versa, provided that the changes in the environment are precisely the sequential processes of the other autonomous units.

There also is a strong connection between the sequential processes of a community $COM = (Goal, InitUnits)$ and the aut-processes of one of its participating units $aut \in Aut$:

$$SEQ(COM) \subset SEQ_{Change(aut)}(aut).$$

For a sequential process $s = (G_0, G_1, \ldots) \in SEM(COM)$ of a community $COM = (Goal, InitUnits)$ only transformations of the participating units are applied in every transformation step, i.e.,

$$(G_i, G_{i+1}) \in \bigcup_{a \in Aut} SEM(P_a)$$

Example Place/Transition Systems

Let $COM(N, m_0)$ be the system of autonomous units that corresponds to a P/T system. Then the application of a rule yields the same effect as the firing of a transition. In this way sequential processes correspond to the firing sequences of the P/T system.

Example Ant Colony

The gathering of food by foraging ants can be regarded as sequential processes in the ant colony model. In every step of such a process a change of the environment occurs, since an ant moves from one field to another. The definition of sequential processes allows for an arbitrary order of the involved ants. This means that it is not guaranteed that the ants move in a consistent way. On the contrary, a sequence of environments where exactly one ant has moved is perfectly legal according to the definition. If a consistent and fair scheduling of the participating units is desired (as would be the case with e.g. board or most card games), additional effort has to be put into the specification of the rules and the environment. An example of such a fair scheduling can be found in Chapter 6, where the board game Ludo is modeled as a community of autonomous units.

As an example, consider the following sequential composition of rule applications starting with a reduced initial environment G_0 as depicted in the upper part of Figure 3.8. For easier reading, let the Ant Units have identifiers equal to the identifiers of their corresponding Ant nodes. In the first step, the Ant Unit a1 applies the rule walkWithoutFood, yielding the graph G_1. The corresponding ant is now located at field f3. It also has memorized the movement from field f0 to field f3 by inserting a corresponding memory edge.

Afterwards, the same unit applies the rule walkWithoutFood again, resulting in the transformed environment G_2. The respective ant is now located on field f4, and the movement has again been memorized. In the next step, the Ant Unit a3 also applies its rule walkWithoutFood, moving the respective ant a3 to the field f1, resulting in the graph G_3. The ant also memorizes this movement. Then the Ant Unit a1 applies its rule walkToFood. The corresponding ant a1 is now located at the food source and prepared to carry some food back to the anthill along the memorized route. This situation can be seen in the graph G_4. Directly afterwards the same unit applies the rule walkWithFood. This yields the graph G_5, where the corresponding ant a1 is located at field f4 and carries food. Additionally, it has removed the respective edge of type memory. In the next step of this example, the Ant Unit a1 applies once again the rule walkWithFood, resulting in the graph G_6. Here the memorized section of the path is removed and the respective ant a1 is located on the field f3, which is adjacent to the anthill. For this reason the final step consists of the application of the rule walkToAntHill by Ant Unit a1.

This step concludes the sample sequential process and yields the environment graph G_7, which depicts the situation where one ant has successfully gathered food and brought it to the anthill, while another ant has just started its journey to find food, and yet another ant is still located at the anthill without having moved. It is noteworthy that the environment G_7 can also be reached by a different order of rule applications, i.e. the one movement of the ant a3 can happen in any step. The graph sequence then looks different, but the final environment G_7 is the same then.

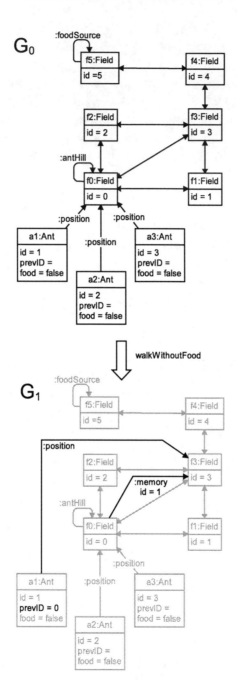

Figure 3.8: Application of rule walkWithoutFood of Ant Unit a1

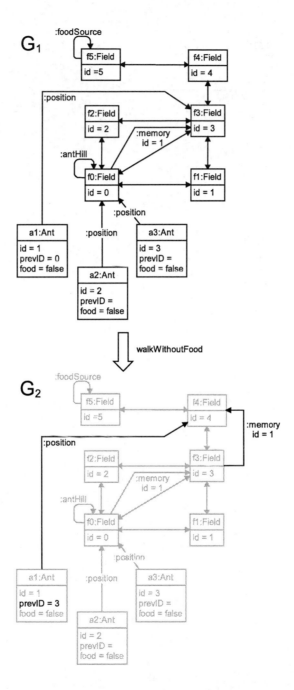

Figure 3.9: Another application of rule walkWithoutFood of Ant Unit a1

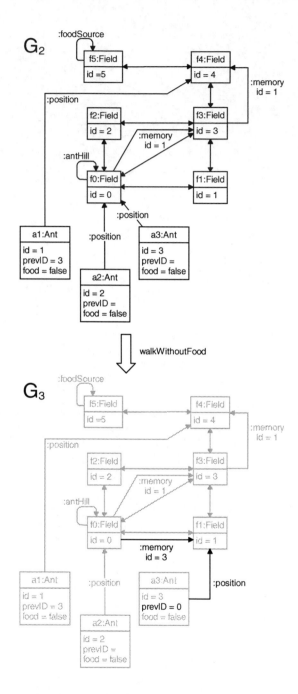

Figure 3.10: Application of rule **walkWithoutFood** of **Ant Unit a3**

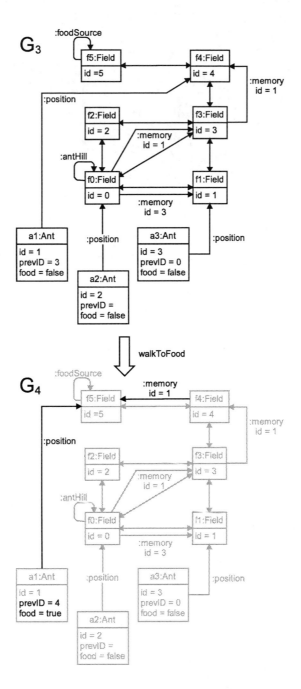

Figure 3.11: Application of rule walkToFood of Ant Unit a1

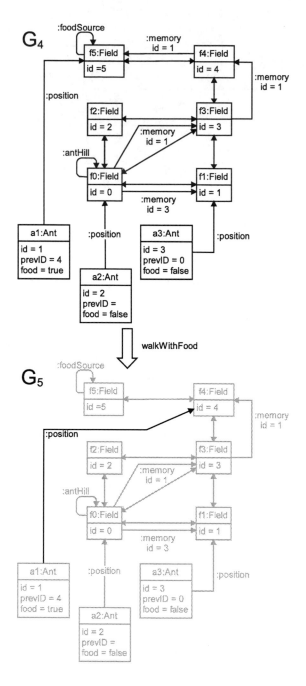

Figure 3.12: Application of rule walkWithFood of Ant Unit a1

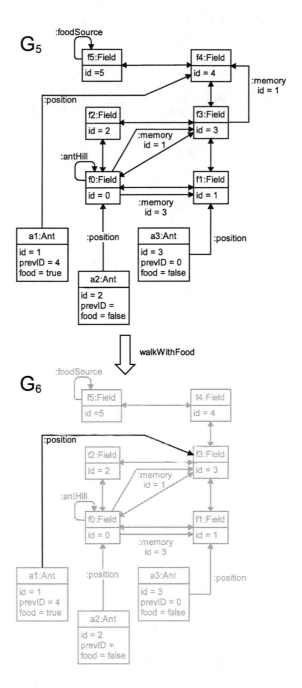

Figure 3.13: Another application of rule walkWithFood of Ant Unit a1

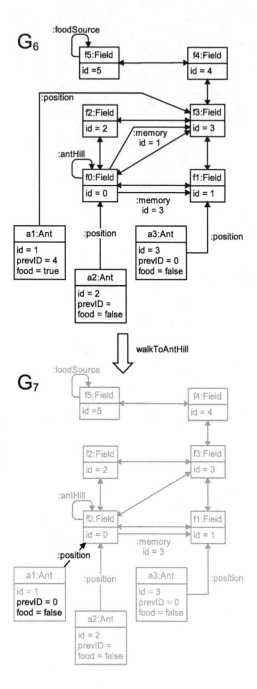

Figure 3.14: Application of rule walkToAntHill of Ant Unit a1

3.3 Parallel Semantics

In most cases it is rather unrealistic to consider a system of processes that transform a shared environment sequentially. The processes in most data processing systems are more suitably modeled by allowing more than one activity on the environment at the same time. This includes in particular the fact that different events, which do not influence each other, can happen in parallel.

The parallel semantics is based on the notion of a parallel graph transformation approach, as specified in Definition 2.2. Because the parallel-process semantics is meant to describe the simultaneous activities of autonomous units, the environment changes must be possible while a single autonomous unit applies its rules. To achieve this, the existence of some rules, called metarules, is assumed, the application of which defines the changes in the environment. Consequently, environment changes and ordinary rules can be applied in parallel. Hence, in the parallel approach a transformation process of an autonomous unit consists of a sequence of parallel rule applications which combine local rule applications with environment changes specified by other components. Every autonomous unit has exactly one thread of control. As in the sequential case, autonomous units regulate their transformation processes by choosing only those rules that are allowed by their control condition in every step.

3.6 Definition (Parallel *aut*-process)
Let $aut = (g, P, c)$ be an autonomous unit and let $Change \subseteq \mathcal{G} \times \mathcal{G}$. Let $\mathcal{MR} \in \mathcal{R}_*$ be a set of parallel rules, called *metarules*, such that $Change = SEM(\mathcal{MR}) = \bigcup_{r \in \mathcal{MR}} SEM(r)$. A *parallel process* of aut with respect to $Change$ is an infinite graph sequence $s = (G_i) \in Seq(\mathcal{G})$ or a finite graph sequence $s = (G_i)_{i \in [n]} \in Seq(\mathcal{G})$ such that

- $(G_{i-1}, G_i) \in SEM(r + r')$ for some $r \in P_*$ and $r' \in \mathcal{MR}$ for $i \in \mathbb{N}_+$ if s is infinite and for $i \in \{1, \ldots, |s|\}$ if s is finite, and

- $s \in SEM_{Change}(c)$.

The set of all parallel aut-processes is denoted $PAR_{Change}(aut)$.

A single step of a parallel aut-process applies a parallel rule of the form $r + r'$ where r is a parallel rule of aut and r' is a metarule. For this reason, the environment graph may undergo additional changes while an autonomous unit acts on it. Please note that r as well as r' may be the null rule, i.e. $r + r' = r$, resp. $r' + r = r'$. Thus one step can also be an exclusive activity of aut or a change of the environment only.

Analogously to the sequential case, a parallel change relation is defined in order to describe the external environment changes. In a closed community, the environment changes that occur besides the changes of a concrete autonomous unit must be activities of the other units participating in the community.

3.7 Definition (Parallel change relation)

Let $COM = (Goal, Init, Aut)$ be a community of autonomous units. Then the *parallel change relation* with respect to aut is given for each $aut \in Aut$ by the parallel rules composed of rules of the autonomous units in COM without aut as metarules, i.e.

$$Change_{\parallel}(aut) = \bigcup_{a \in Aut - \{aut\}} SEM((P_a)_*).$$

Every transformation process of a community must be a parallel aut-process of every autonomous unit aut participating in the community.

3.8 Definition (Parallel process)

Let $COM = (Goal, Init, Aut)$ be a community of autonomous units. A *parallel process* is then defined as a finite or infinite graph sequence $s \in Seq(\mathcal{G})$ such that $s \in PAR_{Change_{\parallel}(aut)}(aut)$ for all $aut \in Aut$.

The parallel processes $PAR(aut), PAR(Init, aut)$ and $PAR(COM) = PAR(Goal, Init, Aut)$ as well as an input-output relation $REL_{PAR}(COM)$ are then obtained analogously to the sequential case.

There is also a strong connection between the parallel processes of a community $COM = (Goal, Init, Aut)$ and the parallel aut-processes of a participating autonomous unit $aut \in Aut$:

$$PAR(COM) \subset PAR_{Change_{\parallel}(aut)}(aut).$$

No autonomous unit can be forced to do anything that is not allowed by its own control: $PAR(COM)$ is the set of all $s \in Seq(\mathcal{G})$ such that $s \in \bigcap_{a \in Aut} PAR_{Change_{\parallel}}(a)$ and $G_0 \in SEM(Init)$ where G_0 is the head of s.

In general, sequential and parallel processes may produce very different results. Consider for instance cellular automata (see, e.g., [Wol02]), where a transition step of all linked finite automata depends on the state of its neighbors. Here a parallel computational step of some automata would change the context of the other automata such that later steps yield different configurations. In other approaches, like e.g. Petri nets, term replacement, or graph transformation, parallel changes do not affect the final output but yield a reduced number of transformation steps. This is due to the fact that the parallel actions may also occur sequentially in an arbitrary order without affecting the final result. This phenomenon is called *true concurrency*. In order to obtain true concurrency in the context of parallel transformation approaches the following has to hold:

Let $R = R' + R''$ be the sum of two multisets of rules and $G \underset{R}{\Rightarrow} X$ be a parallel derivation step. Then parallel derivation steps $G \underset{R'}{\Rightarrow} H$ and $H \underset{R''}{\Rightarrow} X$ exist for a suitable environment H.

Remember that every multiset is the commutative sum of its single elements. For this reason, true concurrency implies that every parallel step could also be executed as an arbitrarily ordered sequence of the corresponding single rule applications, yielding the same result. Parallel processes and their sequentialization are called *equivalent* in the context of concurrency. Consider an equivalence class of a parallel process, i.e. all processes that are equivalent to each other. Then the chronological order of two rule applications can only be determined if one causally depends on the other. Otherwise they can be applied in parallel or in an arbitrarily ordered sequential way.

$SEQ(Aut) \subseteq PAR(Aut)$ is true for the processes of a set of autonomous units Aut. Furthermore, an equivalent process $\bar{s} \in SEQ(Aut)$ can be found for every process $s \in PAR(Aut)$. For a system of autonomous units S this implies in particular

$$REL_{SEQ}(S) = REL_{PAR}(S)$$

in the case of true concurrency.

Example Place/Transition Systems

A parallel transformation approach is obtained by defining parallel firing for a multiset of transitions in a P/T system in the usual way. For the system $COM(N, m_0)$, the parallel processes correspond exactly to the firing sequences of multisets of transitions.

Example Ant Colony

The movement of the foraging ants can also be regarded as parallel processes in the ant colony example. The process step depicted in Figure 3.15 can be regarded as the application of the rule walkWithoutFood of every participating Ant Unit in parallel.

3.4 Concurrent Semantics

Like the sequential process semantics, the parallel process semantics may not be suitable for every application situation. This is due to the fact that components that act autonomously and independently, do not necessarily start and finish their activities simultaneously, as is the case with parallel steps. If such components act far away from each other, or work on completely different tasks without influencing each other it may even not be possible to determine simultaneity. Demanding or enforcing simultaneity would not make any sense in this case anyway. A chronological order of concurrent and distributed processes is only given in the case that one activity needs something that another activity provides. Such causal relationships can be expressed by directed edges between these activities. In the case of concurrent processes this results in an acyclic graph of activities. Such a graph yields a concept for concurrent processes in communities of autonomous units. This is basically the same idea as in the notion of processes of Petri nets.

Let $COM = (Goal, Init, Aut)$ be a system of autonomous units over a parallel transformation approach $\mathcal{A} = (\mathcal{G}, \mathcal{R}, \mathcal{X}, \mathcal{C})$. Then a *concurrent process* consists of an initial environment G_0 and an acyclic, directed graph $run = (V, E, lab)$, with a set of nodes V and a set of edges $E \subseteq V \times V$. The nodes are marked with $lab : V \to \mathcal{R}$, which maps every node to a rule. The following must also hold for G_0 and *run*:

1. Every node in *run* must be reachable via a path originating in an initial node, i.e. a node without incoming edges.

2. Every complete beginning part of *run*, i.e. a subgraph which contains all initial nodes and with every node also all paths from the initial nodes to that node, is either finite or contains an infinite path.

3. For every complete beginning part a parallel process $(G_i)_{i \in N}$ together with a bijection between the nodes of the subgraph and the applied

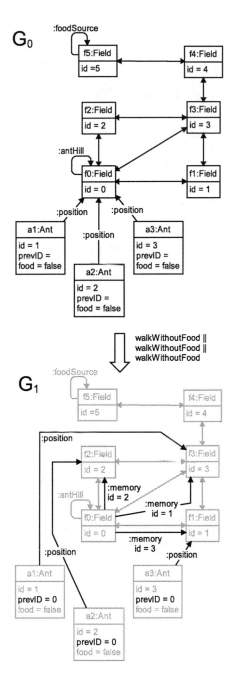

Figure 3.15: Parallel application of rule walkWithoutFood

rules can be found for $N = [n]$, $n \in \mathbb{N}$ or $N = \mathbb{N}$. These rules conform to the markings of the nodes. This bijective relation keeps the causal dependency. This means that a rule which marks the source of an edge in the subgraph is always applied in an earlier step than the rule which marks the target of this edge.

The first condition enforces that *run* does not contain infinite paths without start. Otherwise there would be a path with no corresponding process. The second condition implies that only finitely many nodes are causally independent of each other. The third condition guarantees that concurrent processes are actually executable.

Example Place/Transition Systems

With the notion of occurrence nets at least the special case of *Condition/Event* (*C/E*) nets has a similar process concept. If every path of length 2 that runs along a condition is replaced with a directed edge in such an occurrence net, then a concurrent process in the aforementioned sense is obtained.

Example Ant Colony

The movement of the foraging ants in the ant colony example can happen concurrently, since there are no dependencies between the actions of **Ant Units**.

An elaborated description of the relation between parallel and concurrent processes has to be deferred to future work. It is noteworthy that in the case of true concurrency a strong relation between concurrent processes and canonical derivations exist. This has been investigated in [Kre78] in the context of graph transformation employing the double-pushout approach. Such canonical derivations represent equivalence classes of parallel derivations in a unique way by enforcing maximum parallelity and an application as soon as possible.

3.5 Concluding Remark

In this chapter, communities of autonomous units have been introduced as a means for modeling systems in which different components interact in a rule-based, self-controlled, and goal-driven manner within a common environment. The notion of communities has been illustrated by two example models. On the one hand Petri nets have been modeled as a community of autonomous units where every transition is realized as one autonomous unit. On the other hand a simplified ant colony where every ant is modeled by an autonomous unit has been presented. The autonomous units introduced here provide a sequential, a parallel, and a concurrent process semantics. The former two have been discussed in detail while the latter is only touched on.

As underlying formal framework for communities of autonomous units graph transformation is used. This is highly adequate if the common environment can be represented in a natural way as a graph. Nevertheless, it is worth noting that the graphs and the graph transformation rules the units are working with are not further specified in the underlying graph transformation approach. For this reason any rule-based mechanism that provides a set of configurations and a set of rules specifying a binary relation on such configurations, can serve as formal basis.

Chapter 4

Application: Transport Logistics

Transport logistics deals with the problems of how to transport load from one place to another while minding a set of constraints. Time frames for the delivery have to be kept in mind. The fleet size is restricted and so are the drivers' capacities. In general not only the feasibility of the transport is of importance but also economic constraints. It is a well-known result from graph theory and complexity theory that those scheduling problems are hard to solve. The traveling sales person problem [LK73], for instance, is NP-complete although it seems to be quite simple compared to realistic scenarios. Having small scheduling problems and an idealized environment, the exact solution can be computed in time. But if schedules become large, the run-time of such exact algorithms increases dramatically and makes them practically not applicable. As a result, it is most likely that there is no efficient, exact algorithm computing such tours in a reasonable time. But concerning the transport logistics it is the everyday business of a carrier to schedule trucks that pickup and deliver loads, and return to a depot afterwards. Heuristics that compute good solutions instead of optimal ones are the way out of this dilemma. In [SS95] an introduction to the pickup and delivery problem can be found. The natural representation of a transport net as a graph resulted in first attempts to specify the pickup and delivery scenario with graph transformation rules in [KKK02].

Today, the structural and dynamic complexity of transport networks is increasing. The demands for transports are hardly predictable. If demand changes occur, many plans are invalidated and the scheduling has to start again. Central planning is a bottleneck in the decentralized global world.

A new challenge is to pass autonomy to the actors that have capabilities to adapt to changes at run-time.

In this chapter a methodology similar to those presented in [HKK06a] and [HKK+07] is sketched to formally model transport networks by means of autonomous units that allow for autonomous adaptations. Although formal modeling seems to be extra work load in business it has many advantages. Using formal models one can specify all processes that are valid in a certain transport network where a process is regarded as a sequences of operations. From all valid processes the best one can be chosen. A model additionally facilitates the understanding of each process especially if it has a visual representation. A model allows fast adaptations and algorithms can easily be derived thereof.

An autonomous unit may represent any active component of a logistic system. In the particular context of transport logistics, it represents a vehicle, load, or even an RFID tag. Autonomous units have access to a common environment in which they may cooperate or compete. Depending on the application domain, such an environment can consist of all relevant places, e.g. cities, ports, stations, airports, etc., and relations between them, e.g. roads, railways, waterways, and communication channels. Additionally, in the pickup and delivery scenario the loads and available vehicles are part of the environment.

The autonomous units define the operational capabilities of the components. They run in a potentially nondeterministic way. In general they have a choice when performing the next action. Each unit controls itself autonomously to cut down this non-determinism. It is not controlled from outside. The choice of the next action depends on the type of autonomy specified in the autonomous unit.

4.1   Transport Nets

Roughly speaking, a transport net is a graph with nodes representing places like depots or airports connected by different relations like roads or railways. In this very simple example of the pickup and delivery scenario, the only mode of transport are trucks, and the only relations are roads.

Figure 4.1 shows a small excerpt containing depots in the cities Dortmund, Bremen, Hamburg and Hanover, two trucks with their identifiers (1,2), and a load unit (1). The depots are connected by roads which are labeled with the time that is needed to travel along this connection. The trucks are labeled with a number which represents the amount of hours the truck may travel. In the given example truck 1 is permitted to travel for eight hours, while truck 2 may move around for sixteen hours (because it may be equipped with two drivers). Both truck nodes are connected to a rectangular tour node which is labeled with a number and an exclamation mark. The number defines the payload capacity of the truck, specified in tons in our example. Truck 1 has a payload of 6 tons, and truck 2 is allowed to transport 12 tons. The exclamation mark indicates the current tour node. A package node is labeled with a number which specifies its weight. It is also connected to a rectangular tour node, which in turn is connected to the depot that currently holds the package. Analogously to the truck tour node the exclamation mark indicates the current package tour node. An edge labeled **dest** connects the package node with its destination depot, i.e. the depot to which the package has to be delivered. So in the given situation, truck 1 will start its tour at the depot in Dortmund, and truck 2 will start in Hamburg. The only load unit is currently located at the depot in Dortmund and has to be transported to the depot in Hamburg.

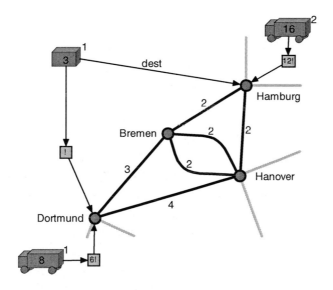

Figure 4.1: A transport net represented by a graph

4.2   Transport Net Graph Model

In this section the type graph of the transport net model is introduced. It is depicted in Figure 4.2.

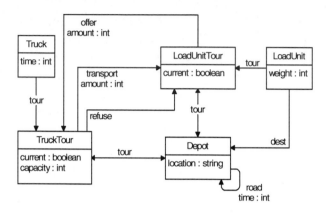

Figure 4.2: The graph model of the transport net specification

A node of type **Depot** with a string attribute **location** represents a depot at that location, a node of type **Truck** with an integer attribute **time** a truck with the corresponding drive time, and a node of type **LoadUnit** a unit load. The load unit has an integer attribute **weight** which holds the weight of the unit load in an appropriate unit, e.g. tons. Nodes of the types **LoadUnitTour** and **TruckTour** are used for the representation of scheduled tour sections. For this reason, they are connected to **Depots** by edges of type **tour** in both directions and to their respective **LoadUnit** and **Truck** nodes. **Depot** nodes are interconnected by edges of type **road** which have an integer attribute **time** representing the estimated time it takes to travel along the road. A **LoadUnit** node is connected to the **Depot** node corresponding to the target location by an edge of type **dest**. A node of type **TruckTour** can be connected to a **LoadUnitTour** node by an edge of type **refuse** or by an edge of type **transport**, which has an integer attribute **amount**. A connection in the reverse direction is possible with an edge of type **offer**, which also has an integer attribute **amount**.

4.3 The Transport Net Community

4.3.1 The Initial Environment

The initial environment of the transport net model consists of nodes of type **Depot** interconnected by **road** edges which store the estimated travel time in their **time** attribute. For every autonomous truck unit a **Truck** node has to be present in the environment connected to one **TruckTour** node which is marked as current. That node is connected to a node of type **Depot**. Analogously, for every autonomous load unit a **LoadUnit** node has to be present which carries the unit load's weight in the **weight** attribute, and is connected to a **LoadUnitTour** node which is marked as current and connected to a node of type **Depot**. As an example, the graph representation of the environment depicted in Figure 4.1 is shown in Figure 4.3.

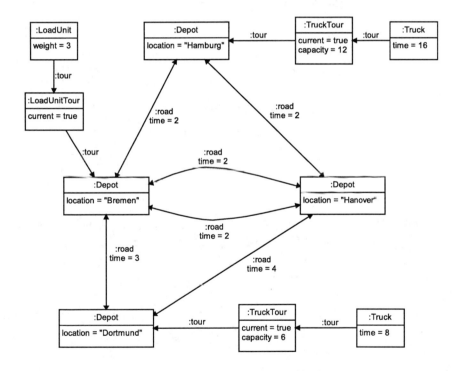

Figure 4.3: A sample initial environment

4.3.2   The Autonomous Unit **Load Unit**

The autonomous unit **Load Unit** models a unit load. It manifests itself in the environment as a node of type **LoadUnit**. This node is referred to as the parameter **lu:LoadUnit** in the name of the unit. This parameter is also needed by the goal and all the rules of this unit. Figure 4.4 shows an overview of the unit.

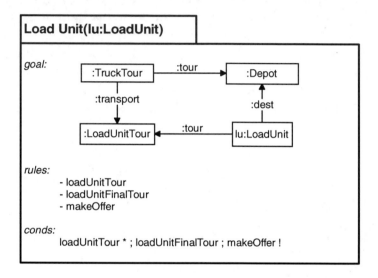

Figure 4.4: The autonomous unit **Load Unit**

The goal of a load unit is to be transported to its destination depot. In the context of this model, that goal is reached once the load unit is scheduled for transport on a tour section of a truck that ends at the destination depot. As can be seen later on, precisely this situation is specified by the goal graph.

The control condition demands to apply the rule **LoadUnitTour** as long as desired. Then the rule **LoadUnitTourFinal** is applied once. After that, the rule **makeOffer** is applied as long as possible.

Figure 4.5 shows the rule **loadUnitTour**.

Its parameter **lu** refers to the manifestation of the corresponding autonomous unit in the environment. This rule extends the tour of a load unit, but only if the next tour section does not already lead to the destination depot. The left-hand side of the rule detects the current **LoadUnitTour** node

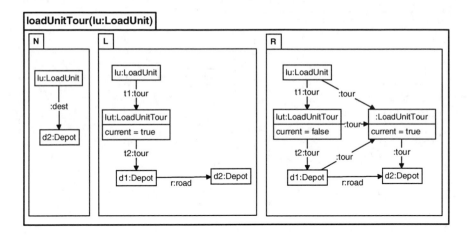

Figure 4.5: Arranging a load unit tour

lut, which should be the only tour node connected to lu with the **current** attribute value **true**. This tour node is connected to a **Depot** node, which is in turn connected to another **Depot** node d2 by a **road** edge. The NAC N forbids the application of this rule if the **Depot** node d2 is already the destination of lu, which is indicated by the **dest** edge connecting lu and d2.

If this rule is applied, a new node of type **LoadUnitTour** is inserted, its **current** attribute value is set to **true**, and it is connected to the nodes d1, d2, lut, and lu by **tour** edges. The tour node lut is no longer the current one, so its corresponding attribute value is set to **false**.

Figure 4.6 shows the rule **loadUnitFinalTour**. Its parameter lu refers to the manifestation of the corresponding autonomous unit in the environment. The purpose of this rule is to finish the tour planning of a load unit. Thus, the left-hand side detects a situation where the current tour node is connected to a depot which is adjacent to the destination depot of the load unit, as indicated by the edge of type **dest** between the corresponding **Depot** node d2 and lu.

If this rule is applied, a new **LoadUnitTour** node is inserted into the environment analogously to the application of rule **loadUnitTour**. But instead of setting the **current** attribute value of the new **loadUnitTour** node to **true**, it is also set to **false**. This is due to the fact that the tour of the load unit is now finished, and thus no current tour node is needed anymore.

Figure 4.7 shows the left-hand side of the rule **makeOffer**. Its parameter lu refers to the manifestation of the corresponding autonomous unit in the

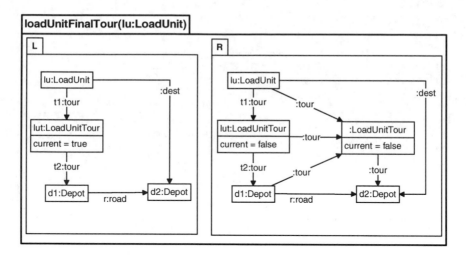

Figure 4.6: The final part of the load unit tour

environment. The left-hand side of this rule detects a situation where a tour section of a truck coincides with a tour section of a load unit. The application condition in the lower left corner of the left-hand side demands that the weight $\_t$ of the load unit lu is less or equal to the payload capacity $\_c$ of the truck for the tour section in question. Additionally, this rule is only applicable for load unit tour nodes that are not marked as current.

Figure 4.8 shows the negative application conditions of this rule. The

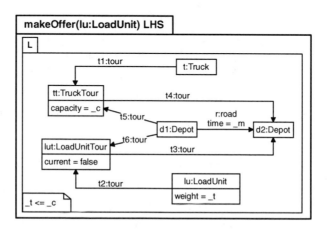

Figure 4.7: Left-hand side of a load unit offer

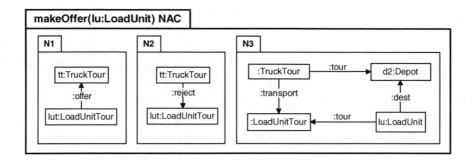

Figure 4.8: NACs of a load unit offer

NAC **N1** ensures that there is no offer yet, while the NAC **N2** ensures that the truck has not yet rejected the offer. The NAC **N3** depicts the same situation as in the goal of the **Load Unit**. If the load unit is scheduled for transport to its destination depot, this rule is not applicable.

Figure 4.9 shows the right-hand side of the rule **makeOffer**. If this rule is applied, a new edge of type **offer** is inserted, connecting the **LoadUnitTour** node with the **TruckTour** node. Its attribute value **amount** is set to _n. The post condition in the lower left corner of the right-hand side indicates that the amount _n of the offer has to be somewhere between 1 and the product of the travel time _m and the weight _t of the package. Thus, a load unit cannot make overstated offers.

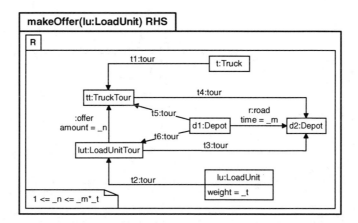

Figure 4.9: Right-hand side of a load unit offer

4.3.3   The Autonomous Unit **Truck Unit**

The autonomous unit **Truck Unit** models a truck. It manifests itself in the environment as a node of type **Truck**. This node is referred to as the parameter **t:Truck** in the name of the unit. This parameter is also needed by all the rules of this unit. Figure 4.10 shows an overview of the unit.

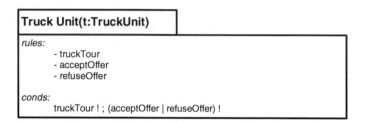

Figure 4.10: The autonomous unit **Truck**

The truck unit has no explicit goal, which means that it allows all graphs as a goal. The control condition demands that the rule **truckTour** is applied as long as possible. Afterwards one of the rules **acceptOffer** and **refuseOffer** may be randomly selected. This selection is repeated as long as possible.

Figure 4.11 shows the rule **truckTour**. Its parameter **t** refers to the manifestation of the corresponding autonomous unit in the environment.

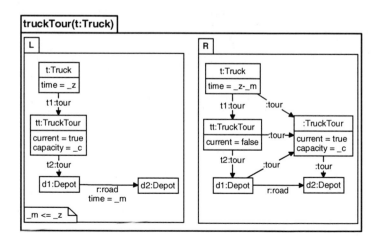

Figure 4.11: Arranging a truck tour

The purpose of this rule is to extend a truck tour as long as there is still moving time left. The left-hand side of the rule detects the current TruckTour node tt, which should be the only tour node connected to t with the current attribute value true. This tour node is connected to a Depot node, which is in turn connected to another Depot node d2 by a road edge. The time for traveling on this road is _m. The time that is left for the truck tour is _z. Thus, this rule can only be applied if _z is greater or equal to the travel time _m, as indicated by the application condition in the lower left corner of the left-hand side.

If this rule is applied, a new node of type TruckTour is inserted, its current attribute value is set to true, its capacity attribute value is set to the same value as the capacity attribute value of tt, and it is connected to the nodes d1, d2, tt, and t by tour edges. The tour node tt is no longer the current one, so its corresponding attribute value is set to false.

Figure 4.12 shows the rule acceptOffer. Its parameter t refers to the manifestation of the corresponding autonomous unit in the environment. This rule models the acceptance of an offer for transportation. This rule is applicable if a load unit lu has made an offer for transportation, which is indicated by the offer edge connecting the LoadUnitTour node lut and the TruckTour node tt. Additionally, the two Depot nodes d1 and d2 that are involved in the tour section corresponding to lut are detected.

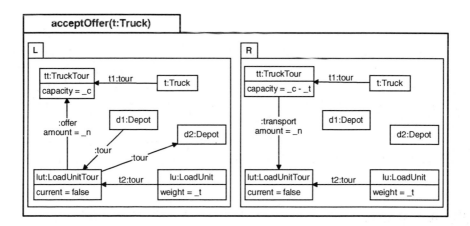

Figure 4.12: Accepting an offer from a load unit

If this rule is applied, the offer edge is replaced by a reversely directed edge of type transport. Its amount attribute value is set to the amount value of the original **offer** edge. Furthermore, the **tour** edges connecting the **Load-UnitTour** node **lut** with the depots **d1** and **d2** are removed, as this information can now be extracted from the truck tour node **tt**. Moreover, this removal also ensures that the package does not make any further offers for this tour section, since the removed edges are needed by the left-hand side of the corresponding offer rule. Additionally, the payload capacity of the truck for this tour section is adjusted by setting the **capacity** attribute value of **tt** to the original value _c minus the weight _t of the load unit now scheduled for transport.

Figure 4.13 shows the rule **refuseOffer**.

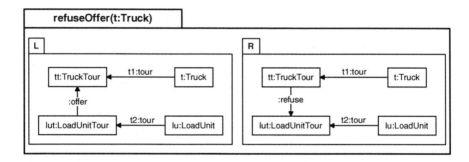

Figure 4.13: Refusing an offer from a load unit

Its parameter **t** refers to the manifestation of the corresponding autonomous unit in the environment. This rule models the refusal of an offer for transportation. This rule is applicable if a load unit **lu** has made an offer for transportation, which is indicated by the **offer** edge connecting the **LoadUnitTour** node **lut** and the **TruckTour** node **tt**.

If this rule is applied, the **offer** edge is replaced by a reversely directed edge of type **refuse**, indicating that the truck has refused to transport the offering load unit.

4.3.4   Sample Derivation

In this section, a sample derivation of the transport net model is presented. The derivation starts with the initial environment as presented in Figure 4.3. Now the **Load Unit** applies its rule **loadUnitTour** in such a way that the tour section leads from **Dortmund** to **Bremen**. Figure 4.14 shows the changes in the environment after the rule application.

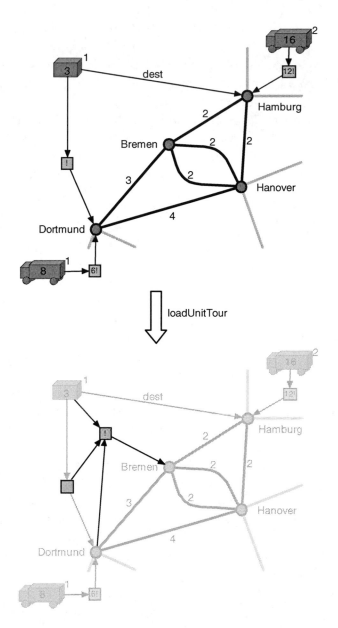

Figure 4.14: Application of rule loadUnitTour

Since the current tour node of the load unit is now connected to a depot which is connected to the destination depot, the rule loadUnitFinalTour is applicable. Its application yields the transformed environment depicted in Figure 4.15.

Now the Truck Unit 1 applies its rule truckTour in such a way, that it adds a tour section from Dortmund to Bremen. Figure 4.16 shows the transformed environment after this rule application.

Omitting Truck Unit 2, two rule applications are now possible. On the one hand, the Truck Unit 1 can extend its tour because there is still movement time left. On the other hand, the tour sections of Truck Unit 1 and the Load Unit coincide on the tour from Dortmund to Bremen. Additionally, the payload capacity of truck 1 is 6, which is greater than the weight 3 of the load unit. Thus, the rule makeOffer of the Load Unit is applicable. The environment after this application might look like the graph depicted in Figure 4.17. Here the amount that is offered by the Load Unit has to satisfy the post condition of the rule, otherwise the offered amount is randomly chosen.

Now the Truck Unit 1 cannot directly react to the offer. Its control condition demands an application of the rule truckTour as long as possible before it can apply acceptOffer or refuseOffer. Since there is still movement time left for the truck, and adjacent depots are reachable in less time, the truckTour rule is still applicable. In the given excerpt of the environment, a number of next tour sections are possible, e.g. from Bremen to Hamburg and then further to Hanover or from Bremen to Hanover and then to Hamburg. It is also possible to directly plan a tour section that leads back to the tour start in Dortmund, since neither the rule specifications nor the control condition would prohibit this. So in this sample derivation, the Truck Unit 1 plans a direct tour back to Dortmund, yielding the environment depicted in Figure 4.18. Now there is still a movement time of 2 left for Truck Unit 1. Thus, it is not possible to expand the tour to Hanover or Bremen. Assuming that the travel time from the depot in Dortmund to any other depot not depicted is also greater than 2, the rule truckTour is now no longer applicable. Thus, the control condition now demands a random choice of one of the rules acceptOffer and refuseOffer, both of which are applicable due to the offer edge of the Load Unit. In this sample derivation, the truck chooses to accept the offer. Thus, the environment is transformed to look like Figure 4.19.

This rule application concludes the sample derivation. The rules have been applied in the following order: loadUnitTour, loadUnitFinalTour, truckTour, makeOffer, truckTour, acceptOffer. Although the control conditions impose

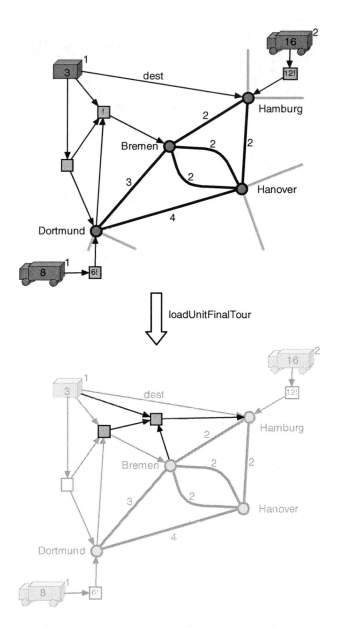

Figure 4.15: Application of rule loadUnitFinalTour

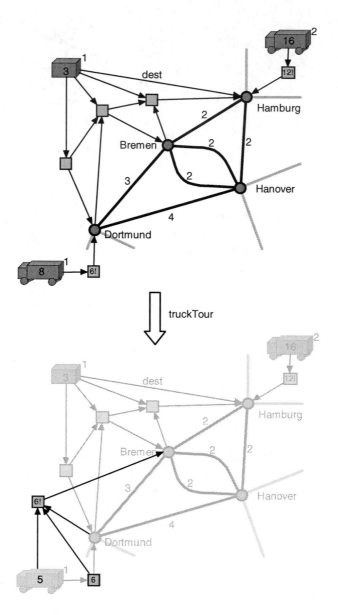

Figure 4.16: Application of rule truckTour

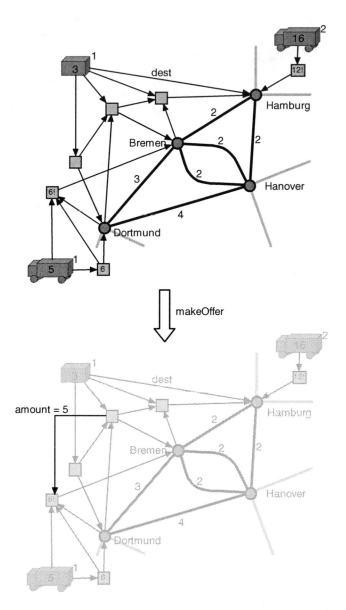

Figure 4.17: Application of rule makeOffer

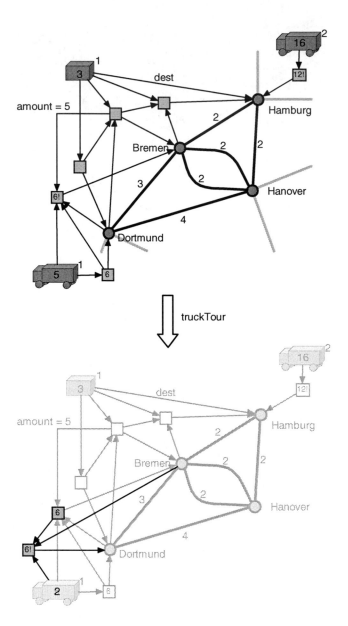

Figure 4.18: Application of rule truckTour

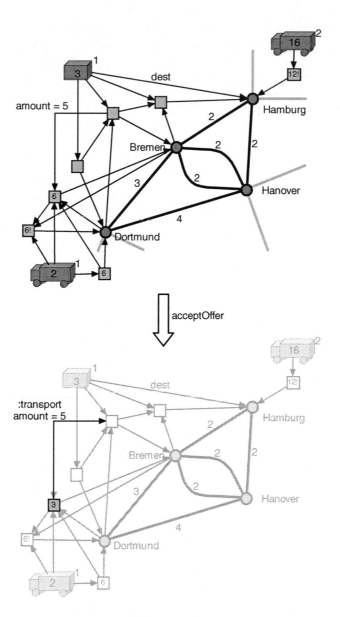

Figure 4.19: Application of rule **acceptOffer**

certain restrictions on the derivation process, a different order of rule applications would yield the same final environment. The tour planning rules of the truck and the unit load can happen in any order and even in parallel. Only the rule makeOffer of the Load Unit demands an already planned and coinciding truck tour section as well as a finished unit load tour planning. Additionally, the rule acceptOffer of the Truck Unit demands an actual offer, thus the rule makeOffer of the Load Unit must have been applied previously.

4.4   Concluding Remark

In this chapter, a simple transport network has been modeled by a community of autonomous units, where every truck and every unit load is realized as an autonomous unit. It has been shown that the rather simple rule set allows for a truck tour plan as well as a load unit tour plan, both of which actually make sense. The load unit is even scheduled to be transported on its first tour section, which also makes some sense. Of course it would be better to choose a truck which also continues to the final destination because of higher costs for transshipping the unit load between trucks. But since no truck is available that meets this condition, the chosen solution at least takes the unit load nearer to its destination depot. It is noteworthy that there is no mechanism in the presented model that ensures a reasonable result. A load unit could e.g. plan nonsensically long tours, and especially the truck's decision concerning acceptance or refusal of an offer happens randomly with equal probability without further reasoning. In order to enforce reasonable results, the basic model presented in this chapter would have to be extended. One step in this direction is to model a more sophisticated negotiation between trucks and load units. This is presented in the next chapter.

Chapter 5

Application: Dynamic Scheduling

In this chapter, a communication-based approach will be introduced, which extends the pickup-and-delivery scenario from Chapter 4 by a more sophisticated negotiation between trucks and load units, and an extended transport net model. In this chapter the scenario is the following: Unit loads arriving at consolidation points for further transportation are queued (see, e.g., [Coo81] for an introduction to queuing theory) according to their arrival time in a first come, first served manner but are scheduled according to their own constraints. Often the order of arrivals is rather arbitrary and does not reflect the real priorities of the transports to be accomplished. In addition, transport orders can arrive at any time, so early scheduling cannot react accordingly. Also, due to limited resources, the simultaneous transport of unit loads can be impossible and can force loads to pause. Imagine a queue of 100 unit loads where only one load at position 98 is having a hard time constraint to be met. Would it not be fair to give this unit load the chance to be served first? In this case the load would have to pay a higher transportation rate while the remaining loads' disadvantages can afterwards be compensated monetarily. In this chapter, a negotiation- and market-based approach is chosen to reorganize the processing of the queue in a decentralized way. For the sake of simplicity, this approach does not take into account the transshipment times.

5.1   Transport Networks

In order to represent time constraints inside the transport network, the model from Chapter 4 has to be adapted. We assume a number of depots in German cities and unit loads (ULDs) to be transported by trucks along road connections from one depot to another one. The main relations of each truck are fixed, i.e. the routing has been arranged in advance as a regular service with timetables for each truck. Based on the knowledge of these timetables, the routes of the ULDs have also been planned in advance. What remains to be scheduled in our scenario is which of the waiting ULDs are actually transported by the respective truck. We propose a negotiation between the truck and the ULDs based on the payment of transportation rates. In this scenario, trucks and ULDs are realized as autonomous units, called truck unit and load unit, respectively. Thus, the underlying environment comprises the consolidation points and their connections. This is modeled as a graph in a straightforward way. Now each truck unit and each load unit becomes part of the environment as a special truck resp. load node. Both kinds of autonomous units utilize tour nodes for a representation of their planned tours (as introduced in [HKL08]. A truck tour is divided into tour sections, which are represented by tour nodes that are connected to the source and target depots of the respective section. These tour nodes are labeled with the estimated time of departure, estimated time of arrival and the capacity for that tour section. A planned load unit tour is represented by tour nodes in a similar way, except for the labels. Load unit tour nodes are labeled with the weight of the ULD and a desired time of arrival (which is n.def in the case that it does not matter when the ULD arrives). Figure 5.1 shows an excerpt of a sample environment.

It contains a truck that has started in Hamburg at noon and drives via Bremen to Dortmund, estimated to arrive at 5pm. There is no capacity left on the first tour section, since the truck transports the load unit lu1 and others (which are not depicted for clarity). The capacity on the second tour section is 8, since it is not yet negotiated which load units are transported on that section. The load unit lu1 with a weight 2 has planned a tour from Hamburg to Dortmund via Bremen, with no fixed arrival time. It is currently being transported from Hamburg to Bremen for a transportation rate of 4 (represented by an accordingly labeled edge between the corresponding tour nodes). Another load unit lu4 with the weight 5 has planned a tour from Bremen to Dortmund with an arrival time not later than 6pm.

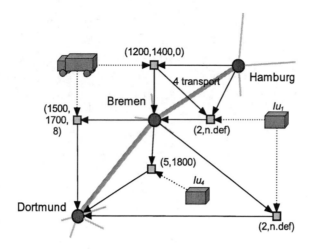

Figure 5.1: Excerpt of a sample transport net

In the next section a sample negotiation based on communication is presented in the form of valid environment derivation steps.

5.2 Sample Negotiation

Consider the following concrete situation. A truck with a load capacity of 8 has recently started its journey from Hamburg to Dortmund via Bremen, transporting different ULDs. One of these is lu1, which has a weight of 2 and is scheduled for further transport to Dortmund, while all the others are unloaded in Bremen. Additionally three load units lu2, lu3, and lu4 with the respective weights 4, 2, and 5, are queued for pickup in Bremen for transportation to Dortmund (here the position in the waiting queue is represented by the indices, in the environment the queue is represented by corresponding queue edges between the load unit nodes). ULDs are queued in the order of their arrival at the consolidation point, resp. the arrival of the corresponding transport order, preferring those ULDs that are already loaded on a truck.

Now each load unit may make an offer for transportation to the desired truck unit. The standard transportation rate in our simplified scenario is calculated to be the weight of the load unit multiplied by the transport time for the tour section in hours given by the timetable (so lu2 would offer a rate of $4 \cdot 2 = 8$). The offer is inserted into the environment by a graph transformation rule, which inserts an edge from the respective tour node of the load unit to the corresponding tour node of the truck unit, labeled with the actual offer and a question mark. These offers have to be made until the truck arrives at the consolidation point where the ULDs are queued. The graph in Figure 5.2 shows an excerpt of the sample environment after all load units that desire transportation from Bremen to Dortmund have made their offers.

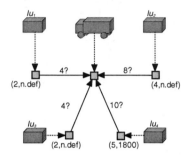

Figure 5.2: Offers of the load units

When the truck arrives at the consolidation point in Bremen, the corresponding truck unit scans the offers of the load units respecting the queue order. In the concrete example, it will accept the ULDs lu1, lu2, and lu3, which will pay the overall rate of **16** and moreover result in a full truckload. Technically this is achieved by a truck rule, which considers the offers of each load unit according to their position in the queue. This rule is applicable, if the weight of a load unit is below or equal to the remaining capacity of the tour section under consideration (skipping every load unit with a weight that exceeds the currently remaining capacity for the tour section). When applied, the rule replaces the edge labeled with the offer by a reversely directed edge labeled with the same offer and an exclamation mark. If the rule is not applicable anymore then there is not enough capacity left for additional load units. The rejection of offers for those load units is handled by a truck rule, which replaces all remaining offer edges with reversely directed edges labeled with the same offer and **#**. This is depicted in Figure 5.3.

In the next step each load unit answers to the accepted or rejected offer. If a unit accepts the truck's decision it labels the corresponding edge with an additional **OK**. If it does not accept the decision of the truck, it labels the corresponding edge with an additional **Not OK**. In our example, lu4 would not accept the decision, as it has to be transported by the considered truck

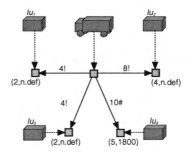

Figure 5.3: Offers of the truck unit

in order to arrive in Dortmund on time. Figure 5.4 shows the situation in the environment after each load unit has commented on the decision of the truck unit.

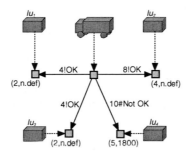

Figure 5.4: Comments of the load units

The truck unit may now fix the transportation schedule if all edges are labeled with **OK**. If an edge is labeled as **Not OK**, then the truck unit may calculate a new rate for the transportation of the corresponding load unit based on the potential rejection of other load units. The necessary amount to be paid is calculated by the truck as the missing amount compared to the full truckload plus one for every previously accepted load unit that now has to be rejected. This additional amount would then be paid to the now rejected load units, so that they would gain a small advantage for further negotiations. In the concrete example, the transportation of lu4 with a weight of 5 would only be possible by likewise rejecting lu2 and lu3, resulting in an overall payment loss of 2 and the usually desired full truckload. In the given scenario, there is no chance to transport lu4 and get a full truckload. The necessary amount to pay for lu4 is now calculated by the truck in the following way. In order to transport lu4, the load unit lu2 definitely has to be rejected due to its weight. Because the load unit lu1 is considered first in the queue (since it is already loaded onto the truck), the load unit lu3 will also be rejected. This yields enough capacity on the truck to transport lu4. The payment rate of lu1 is 4, a full truckload would amount to an overall transportation rate of 16 (the capacity of 8 multiplied by 2 hours). Therefore, the load unit lu4 will have to pay a rate of 12 for compensating the difference compared to the full truckload, and additionally one for every previously accepted and now rejected load unit, in this case 2. Therefore, the overall sum in this example would be 14. The much higher cost of 14 compared to 10 can be justified by the fact that this load unit has a higher urgency and is waiting for a much shorter time (as can be seen by its position in the waiting queue). Technically the rule of the truck unit handling this situation would replace the label of the corresponding edge with the calculated amount and a question mark (the direction of the edge makes it distinguishable from a load unit's offer). It would also mark the potential load units to reject with a loop labeled toReject. Figure 5.5 depicts this situation.

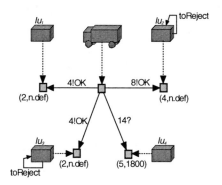

Figure 5.5: New offer of the truck unit

If the load unit does not accept the suggested payment, it would again add Not OK to the suggested amount. This would end the negotiation and lead to the transportation of lu1, lu2, and lu3. If the load unit accepts the suggested payment, which is the case in our example, it can apply a rule which adds OK to the suggested amount. This is depicted in Figure 5.6.

This in turn makes a rule of the truck unit applicable, which replaces the corresponding question mark by an exclamation mark. It also marks the

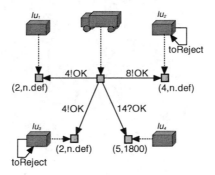

Figure 5.6: Accepting the new offer

previously flagged load units as rejected by replacing !OK with # in their
corresponding edge labels and removing the loop edges labeled toReject.
The situation of the concrete scenario is depicted in Figure 5.7.

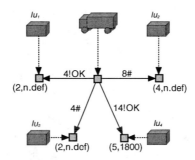

Figure 5.7: New truck offers

Now every rejected load unit again comments on the new decision by
adding OK or Not OK to the corresponding edge labels. In the case of
the concrete scenario, lu2 and lu3 would accept the truck's new decision
because they have no fixed arrival time and thus can wait for a later truck.
Figure 5.8 shows this situation.

In this case, the negotiation is considered finished which is handled by
a rule of the truck unit. Applying this rule labels the edges connecting the
truck tour node and the tour nodes of the transported load units with the
negotiated transport rate and additionally transport. The edges connecting
the truck unit's tour node and the tour nodes of the rejected load units'
tour nodes are removed. Figure 5.9 shows this situation.

If, however, a previously accepted and now rejected load unit had dis-

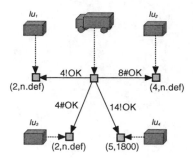

Figure 5.8: Comments of the load units to the new truck offers

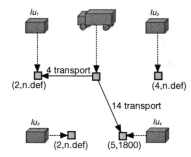

Figure 5.9: Finishing the negotiation

agreed with the new situation, it would again have added **Not OK** to the respective edge label. Then the truck would in turn recalculate the now necessary amount to overrule the current proposition. This recalculation is done as before plus one for every negotiation round in order to avoid repeated transportation rates. An endless negotiation is not possible due to the fact that the transportation rates are increasing with every negotiation round and every load unit has only a fixed amount at its disposal (and is of course not allowed to accept a transport rate which exceeds its own budget). An alternative could be the restriction to a maximum number of offer and accept/reject steps.

5.3 Concluding Remark

In this chapter, an approach to the intelligent scheduling of transports using communicating autonomous units has been presented. Here communication is modeled by the insertion and deletion of edges in the common environment. Although the negotiation is still very simple and does not consider aspects like customer retention, transshipment costs, and competition between different logistic companies it has been shown that a more complex negotiation can be modeled by autonomous units.

Autonomous units are a formal framework still under development. One aim is to use the formal framework to prove properties of the system and its components in general. An interesting aspect to prove in the context of the mentioned situations is the fact that every load unit will be transported to its final destination in time (provided that the overall constraints like capacities and timetables permit this).

Chapter 6

Case Study: Ludo

In this chapter the German variant Don't Get Angry of the board game *Ludo* is modeled using a community of autonomous units. An excerpt of such a model has been introduced in [HKK06b] and implemented and simulated using the graph transformation tool AGG [ERT99]. Since the performance of AGG is rather weak (a single game of Ludo takes more than ten minutes on an average modern machine), the rather new alternative tool GrGen [GBG⁺06] is used here. It is noteworthy that both tools do not support the concept of autonomous units, but provide a convenient interface to their underlying graph transformation engines.

6.1 Don't get angry - A Ludo Variant

Don't Get Angry is a variant of the board game Ludo, which is a simplified version of the traditional Indian game Pachisi. The main difference between Ludo and Don't Get Angry is the fact that they are played on boards with a different layout[1]. The board on which our Ludo variant is played is depicted in Figure 6.1. The track consists of circular fields in the shape of a cross, where each arm is divided into three columns. The middle columns consist of colored fields, which are called target fields, and belong to the player with the same color. The bigger colored circles in the four corners of the board are the homes of the corresponding players. The single, colored fields on the track are the starting fields of the corresponding player.

Ludo can be played by two to four players and is based on rolling a single, six-sided die. The aim of the game is to move all four tokens in a

---

[1]Although Don't Get Angry is a variant of Ludo, the game will hence be called *Ludo* for aesthetic reasons.

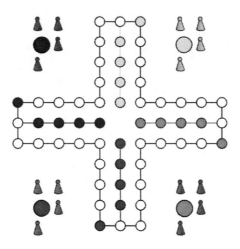

Figure 6.1: Board of Don't Get Angry

clockwise direction from the starting field to the target fields according to the score on the die. The first player having moved all four tokens to their respective target fields wins.

Each player chooses red, green, yellow or blue as their color and places their accordingly colored four tokens near the corresponding home. Every player then rolls a single die and the player with the highest throw starts the game.

Players take turns in a clockwise manner. Throwing 6 always gives another turn. If no legal move is possible, the die is passed to the next player.

Tokens are moved in a clockwise direction on the track according to the score on the die. Tokens may not be moved on fields which are already occupied by a token of the same color. Tokens may also not be moved on home fields of a different color. On throwing 6, a player has to move a token from its home to the starting field. If another token of the same color is already blocking the starting field, it has to be moved away. In general, whenever there are pieces at home, the corresponding starting field has to be cleared as soon as possible. Tokens may jump over other tokens. If a token is moved to a field occupied by a piece of a different color, the latter one is removed from the track and placed at its corresponding home. If more than one token on the track can legally move, the player may freely decide which one they want to take.

6.2 Graph Transformation and **GrGen**

GrGen has been developed as a high performance tool in order to make graph transformation feasible in practical applications. As has been shown in [GBG+06] it is a theoretically sound, fast and easy to use tool.

The allowed node and edge types as well as the attributes associated with each type are defined in a meta model, which corresponds to the type graphs as introduced in Section 2.2. The meta model and the graph transformation rules can be defined separately, thus permitting the use of different rule sets with the same meta model. **GrGen** implements an extension of the well-founded single-pushout (SPO) approach (cf., e.g., [EHK+97]) similar to the approach presented in Section 2.3, but is still very close to the original theory.

The main difference of the approach used so far in this thesis and the approach implemented in **GrGen** is the necessary extension of the original theory in order to incorporate node and edge inheritance. As stated earlier, **GrGen** also provides a convenient user interface to the actual graph transformation engine. Thus it can be used for the simulation of a community of autonomous units with some additional effort.

6.3 Ludo Graph Model

In this section the type graph of the underlying graphs of the game Ludo is introduced. It is depicted in Figure 6.2. Please note that the type graph contains inheritance, which is a feature of the used engine **GrGen**. In a **GrGen** specification it is possible to specify inheritance relations which are obeyed in the matching process. In this model, the node type **Target** is specified to be a subtype of the node type **Field**, which is called its *supertype*. The subtype inherits all attributes and all edge connections from its supertype. In the rule application, a subtype matches a supertype. In this case a node type **Target** matches a node type **Field**. It is noteworthy that this feature is used here only as a shortcut. Without the inheritance feature, almost every rule involving **Field** nodes has to be specified in a similar way with nodes of type **Target** instead of type **Field**.

The specified node types comprise a node type **Die**, which represents the actual die of the game. The node type **Value** represents the score of the die via its integer attribute **v**. The Ludo graph will thus comprise one **Die** node and six **Value** nodes, the latter containing attribute values **v** ranging from 1 to 6, in order to simulate a six-sided die. The node type

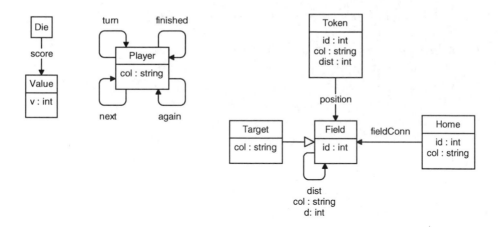

Figure 6.2: Type graph of Ludo

Player represents a participant of the game, the attribute **col** indicating their chosen color. The node type **Field** represents a field on the track. Its attribute **id** holds a unique numerical field identifier, which serves no purpose in the actual graph transformation specification, but is used for layout purposes while drawing the graph (the position of the respective field can directly be derived from its identifier). This node type is extended by the **Target** node type, which represents a target field on the board. Its attribute **col** determines its color. The attribute **id** is inherited from the base type and also serves layout purposes only.

The node type **Token** represents a token that is moved along the track. Its attribute **col** determines its color, **id** its unique identifier in the context of the corresponding color, and **dist** stores the distance in field steps that has been covered by this token so far. As with the **Field** node types the attribute **id** serves only layout purposes while drawing the graph. Finally the node type **Home** represents a home field. Its attribute **col** determines the corresponding token and player color and **id** is an identifier used for layout purposes. A **score** edge connects the **Die** with a **Value** node, representing the number that has been thrown by rolling the die. A player can have three different loop edges. The **finished** edge indicates that the current player has finished their move. The **again** edge indicates that the current player has to roll the die again. The **turn** edge indicates that the corresponding player has to roll the die or has just rolled it but not moved a token yet. The **next** edge connects two different **Player** nodes in order to determine the order in which the game is played. An edge of type **fieldConn** connects a

Home node to a Field node. A Token node is connected to a Field node by
an edge of type position, indicating the current position of the token on the
board. Field nodes also have loop edges of type dist. Every Field node has
four loop edges of this type, one for each color. These loop edges are used
to determine the distance from the start field of the corresponding color.
This information allows for the direct calculation of the field a token can
be moved to. This will be explained in detail later during the discussion of
the actual graph transformation rules.

6.4 The Ludo Community

6.4.1 The Initial Environment

The initial environment graph of the Ludo specification contains the forty
fields of the track, represented as nodes of type Field (hence called field
nodes) with identifiers ranging from 0 to 39. Every field node has four loop
edges of type dist with the col attribute values blue, yellow, green and red,
respectively. For every field with identifier $0 \leq n < 40$ the loop edge with
the value blue has the d attribute value n, the yellow loop edge the value
$(n + 30)$ *modulo* 40, green $(n + 20)$ *modulo* 40 and red $(n + 10)$ *modulo* 40.
The target fields are represented as 16 nodes of type Target with identifiers
ranging from 40 to 55. The target nodes with the identifiers 40 to 43 have
the col attribute value blue, those with 44 to 47 yellow, 48 to 51 green, and
52 to 55 red. Each target node has one loop edge of type dist with the col
attribute value equal to the col attribute value of the node. The d attribute
value of a blue target node with the identifier n is n. The one of a yellow
target node is $40 + (n \ modulo \ 44)$, green $40 + (n \ modulo \ 48)$, and red $40 + (n
\ modulo \ 52)$.

Four nodes of type Home with the respective col attribute values blue,
yellow, green, and red and the respective Id attribute values 56, 57, 58, and
59 correspond to the four home fields. Edges of type fieldCon connect the
home nodes to the respective starting field nodes, i.e. the red home node
to the field node with the identifier 0, the green one to 10, blue to 20 and
yellow to 30. Figure 6.3 shows an excerpt of the initial environment graph
with the yellow home node, two yellow target nodes and three field nodes of
the track with their respective loop edges. Nodes are notated as rectangles,
and edges as arrows. The upper compartment of a node consists of a colon
followed by the type of the node. The lower compartment contains the
attribute names and the current attribute values. Analogously the labels

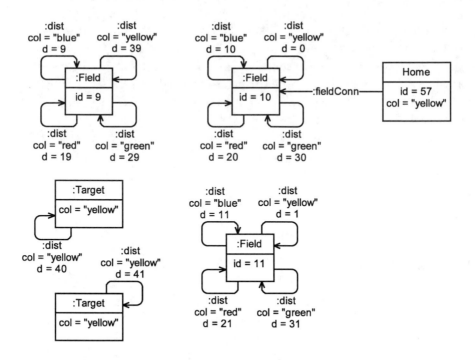

Figure 6.3: An excerpt of the initial Ludo environment

near arrows show the type name of the edge after a colon and the attribute names and their current values below that.

Four **Player** nodes represent the participants of the game. Their **col** attribute has the value blue, yellow, green, and red, respectively. They are connected in a clockwise manner by an edge of type **next**. The die node corresponds to the die of the game and six value nodes to each score that can be rolled. Thus the first value node has the **v** attribute value 1, the second 2, and so on. Figure 6.4 shows an excerpt of the initial environment graph with the four player nodes, the die node and the six value nodes.

Finally, there are four token nodes representing the tokens that can be moved for each of the colors blue, yellow, green, red. Their **col** attribute value is set to their respective color. The first token node of each color has the **id** attribute value 1, the second 2, and so on. The **dist** attribute value of every token node is 0.

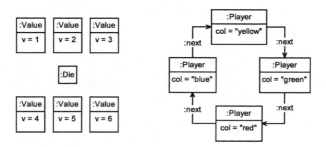

Figure 6.4: Player nodes, die node and value nodes of the initial Ludo environment

6.4.2 The Autonomous Unit **Die**

The autonomous unit Die corresponds to the die of the Ludo game and is depicted in Figure 6.5.

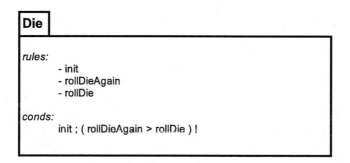

Figure 6.5: The Die unit

Its purpose is to initialize the game by determining a random start player and to throw the die in the course of the game. The Die unit has no explicit goal, i.e. it admits every graph as a goal. The control condition is init;(rollDieAgain>rollDie)!, which is a sequence (as indicated by the semicolon) of the two control conditions init and (rollDieAgain>rollDie)!. The second control condition is a priority condition. It means that if the rule rollDieAgain is applicable, it has to be applied. Only if it is not applicable the lower prioritized rule rollDie has to be applied. The exclamation mark behind the surrounding braces means that the control condition inside the braces has to be applied as long as possible, i.e. until it is not applicable any more. So the control condition of the Die unit specifies that the rule init has to be applied first, and only once. This rule is depicted in Figure 6.6.

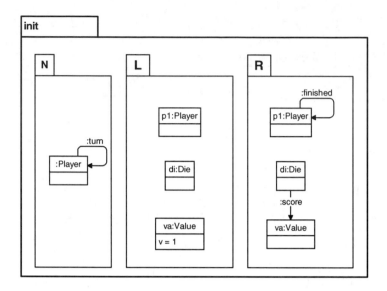

Figure 6.6: The rule init of the Die unit

The rule init randomly chooses a **Player** node and marks it with a **finished** loop. It also connects the **Value** node with the **Die** node, indicating the roll of a 1. This rule is not applicable if there is any **Player** node that is marked with a **turn** edge, as specified in the NAC **N**. This rule actually determines the player before the player who starts the game. This is done in order to use the same die rolling rules for the starting player as those used in the course of the game.

Figure 6.7 depicts the rule **rollDieAgain**.

This rule is applicable if a **Player** node is marked with a **finished** loop edge and a 6 has been rolled. The left-hand side also determines the new score of the die. The shadows beyond the **Value** node rectangles indicate a homomorphic matching, i.e. they may be identical. This is due to the fact that **GrGen** uses injective matching by default. If graph elements may be identified by the match, they need an explicit mark. Without the homomorphic specification, it would be impossible to roll two scores of 6 successively. The application of this rule replaces the **finished** loop with a **turn** loop, indicating that it is still the turn of the corresponding player. The **Die** is connected to the **Value** node representing the new score that has

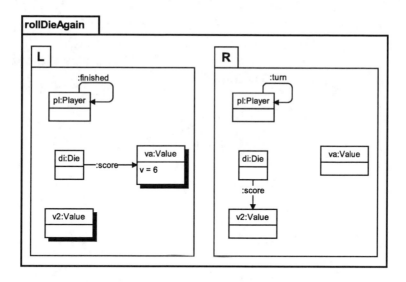

Figure 6.7: The rule rollDieAgain of the Die unit

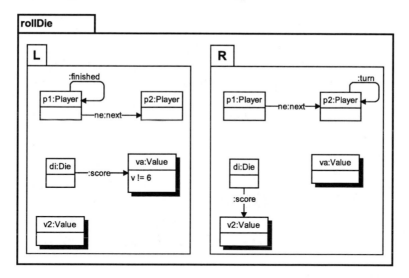

Figure 6.8: The rule rollDie of the Die unit

been thrown.

Figure 6.8 shows the rule rollDie.

In contrast to rule rollDieAgain which is only applicable if a score of 6 has been rolled, this rule demands the score to be different from 6. This is specified in the attribute compartment of the node va by the restriction v != 6. Analogously to the previous rule a new score (that may again be the same score as before) is determined. But in this case, it is the turn of the next player, who is determined in the left-hand side and marked with a turn loop edge by the application of this rule.

6.4.3   The Autonomous Unit **GentlePlayer**

The autonomous unit GentlePlayer models a player who moves the tokens in such a way that knock outs of foreign tokens are avoided whenever possible. Figure 6.9 provides an overview of the unit.

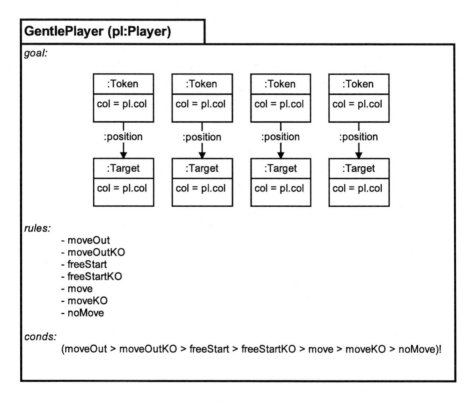

Figure 6.9: The GentlePlayer unit

An autonomous unit that models a player manifests itself in the environment as a node of type **Player**. This node is refered to as the parameter pl:Player in the name of the unit. The goal of the GentlePlayer unit is reached if all tokens that have the same color color as the player have been moved on to the target fields. This is denoted in the figure by the corresponding

col attribute values of the **Token** and **Target** nodes, which have to be equal
to the player's color (referenced by**pl.col**). The control condition is specified
as an *as-long-as-possible* loop over a subcondition that is based on priorities, sorted from left to right. The control condition means that a step as
specified by the subcondition in brackets has to be repeated as long as this
is possible. The subcondition is a list of prioritized rules, meaning that the
first rule **moveOut** has to be applied if possible. If it is not applicable, the
second rule **moveOutKO** has to be applied, and so on. So in every step of
such a unit one of the rules is applied according to the priorities, and these
steps are repeated until none of the rules are applicable, or indefinitely if
there always is at least one rule that can be applied.

Figure 6.10 shows the rule **moveOut** of the **GentlePlayer** unit.

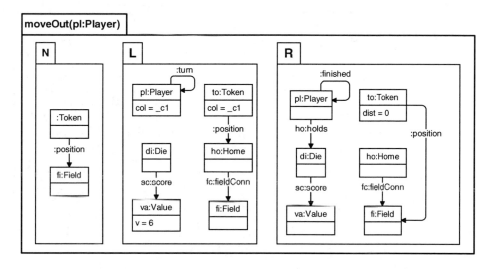

Figure 6.10: The rule **moveOut** of the **GentlePlayer** unit

This rule has a node of type **Player** as a parameter with the name **pl**, as
indicated in braces in the rule name. This is the **Player** node corresponding
to the parameter of the whole autonomous unit. The left-hand side detects
the following situation: it is the turn of the player, the score of the die is 6,
and a token belonging to the player is still on its home field. In this case,
the token has to be moved on the corresponding start field of the track,
provided that no other token is already located there. In the environment
graph the **Field** node connected to the **Home** node by the **fieldConn** edge
refers to that start field. The NAC ensures that no other token is located

on the start field. If this rule is applied, the turn edge is replaced with an edge of type finished, the position edge connecting the Token node to the Home node is deleted, and a new position edge connecting the Token node with the Field node is inserted. Additionally, the dist attribute of the Token node is set to 0, indicating that this token has not yet covered any distance.

Now the situation is considered where the player wants to move out, but a token belonging to a different player is located at the start field. In this case the player needs to move out, knocking the foreign token out. But the NAC prohibits the application of the rule moveOut. For this reason, the rule moveOutKO, depicted in Figure 6.11 is applicable in a situation like this.

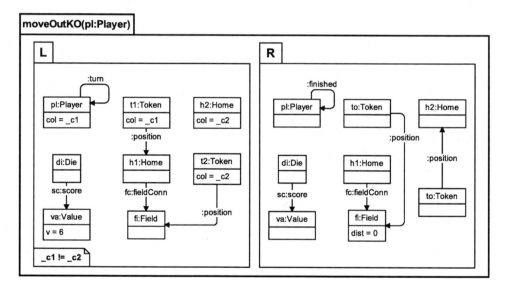

Figure 6.11: The rule moveOutKO of the GentlePlayer unit

In this rule, the left-hand side detects the same situation as in the rule moveOut. Additionally, a foreign token is located at the start field. This is denoted by the attribute condition _c1 != _c2 in the rectangle located in the lower left corner of L, which means that in order for the rule to be applicable, the values of the variables _c1 and _c2 have to be different. Furthermore the home field of the foreign token is determined. An NAC is not necessary in this case, because there should only be at most one token located at a field at any given time during the game. The application of this rule yields the same changes in the environment as the application of the rule **moveOut**. Additionally, the **position** edge connecting the foreign **Token** node to the **Field** node is deleted, and a new **position** edge connecting the node t1 to its **Home** node is inserted.

If a player wants to move out, but the start field is blocked by a different token of the same player, it is not possible to move out. In this case it may be possible to free the start field. This is accomplished by the rule **freeStart**, which is depicted in Figure 6.12.

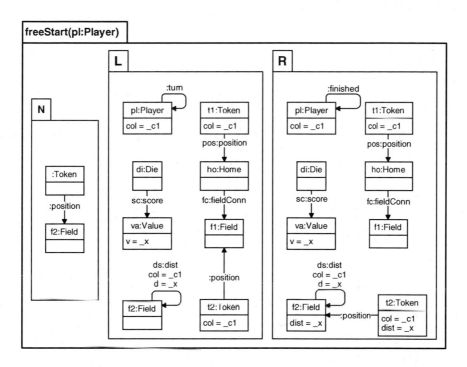

Figure 6.12: The rule **FreeStart** of the **GentlePlayer** unit

The left-hand side of this rule detects the following situation: it is the player's turn, and one of the player's tokens is still at its home field, while another one is located on the start field. In this case, a player has to free the start field if possible. Additionally, the die shows a score of $\_x$. Furthermore, the destination field to which the token currently located at the start field can move with the current score is determined. This is done using the **dist** loop edge **ds** of the corresponding **Field** node f2. Its attribute value **col** matches the player's color and its attribute value **d** carries the distance in fields from the starting field. The NAC ensures that no other token is already located at the destination field. If this rule is applied, the turn edge of the Player node is replaced by an edge of type finished, the position edge connecting the Token node t2 to the Field node f1 is deleted, and a new position edge connecting t2 to f2 is inserted. Furthermore, the dist attribute value of the node t2 is set to _x, which is the distance that the corresponding token has actually covered.

This rule cannot be applied if the destination field is already occupied by a token. If this token is a foreign one, the rule freeStartKO, which is depicted in Figure 6.13, can be applied.

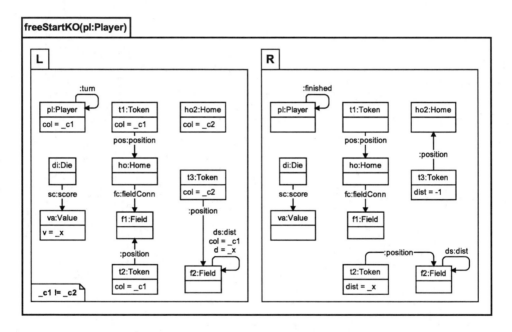

Figure 6.13: The rule FreeStartKO of the GentlePlayer unit

Its left-hand side detects the same situation as in the rule freeStart. Additionally, a foreign token is located at the destination field, denoted again by the attribute condition _c1 != _c2. The home field of the foreign token is also identified. Applying this rule yields the same changes as the application of the rule freeStart, but additionally the foreign token is returned to its home field. This is done by deleting the position edge connecting t3 and f2, and inserting a new position edge connecting t3 and ho2.

The rule move, which is depicted in Figure 6.14, models a simple move of a token without knocking out foreign tokens.

The left-hand side of this rule detects the following situation: it is

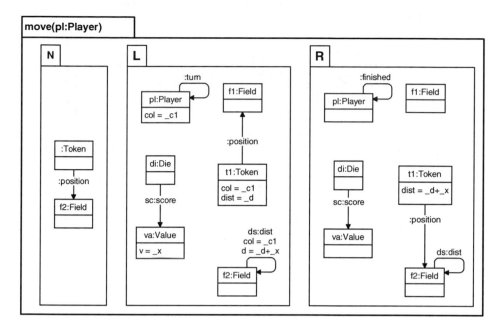

Figure 6.14: The rule **Move** of the **GentlePlayer** unit

the player's turn, the score of the die is _x, and a token of the player
is located somewhere on the track. Furthermore, the destination field to
which the token can move with the current score is determined. This is done
analogously to the method in the previous two rules, but since the token is
not located at the start field, the **d** attribute value of the destination field is
calculated differently. It equals the sum of the distance the corresponding
token has currently covered plus the score of the die. The NAC ensures
that the rule is not applicable if any token is located at the destination
field. If this rule is applied, the **turn** edge of the **Player** node is replaced
by an edge of type **finished**, the **position** edge connecting **t1** to **f1** is deleted,
and a new **position** edge is inserted, connecting **t1** with **f2**. Furthermore, the
distance of the token refered to by **t1** is recalculated to the sum of the old
distance plus the score of the die.

Again, this rule is not applicable if the destination field is occupied by
a foreign token. In this case the rule **moveKO**, depicted in Figure 6.15, can
be applied. It works analogously to the previous rules which handle the
knock outs of foreign tokens.

Finally, there is only one situation left for a complete ludo player. It
may be the case that no move is possible, e.g. if all tokens are at their home

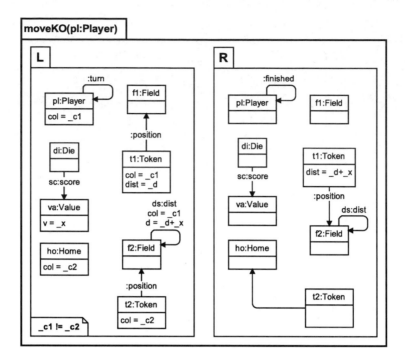

Figure 6.15: The rule MoveKO of the GentlePlayer unit

fields and a score different from 6 has been rolled. In this case, the rule noMove, which is depicted in Figure 6.16, is applied.

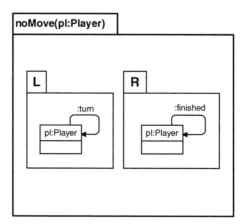

Figure 6.16: The rule NoMove of the GentlePlayer unit

Since this rule has the lowest priority, it can only be applied if all other rules cannot be applied. In this case, the player's turn ends without a move, because no legal move is possible. Thus the rule simply replaces the **turn** loop edge of the **Player** node with a loop edge of type **finished**.

This rule completes the autonomous unit **GentlePlayer**. It models a gentle player, because the priority of moving tokens without knocking out other tokens is higher than that of moving with knocking out. A gentle player only knocks out foreign tokens when there is no other possible move. In the next section, the opposite strategy is specified, i.e. a player knocks out foreign tokens whenever the chance arises.

6.4.4 The Autonomous Unit **AggressivePlayer**

The autonomous unit **AggressivePlayer**, which is depicted in Figure 6.17, models a player which knocks out foreign tokens whenever possible.

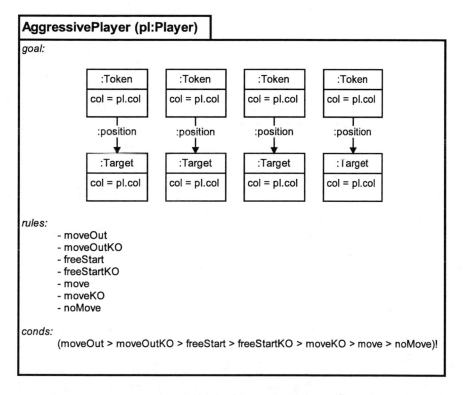

Figure 6.17: The **AggressivePlayer** unit

This unit has the same goal and the same rules as the GentlePlayer
unit. The aggressive playing style is accomplished by simply changing the
priorities of the two rules move and moveKO. If a situation occurs where at
least one move would knock out a foreign token, this move is chosen (unless
the moveOut and freeStart rule variants are applicable of course). It is rather
interesting to see that a completely opposite strategy can be implemented
by simply changing the priority order of two rules.

6.4.5 The Autonomous Unit FastPlayer

The autonomous unit FastPlayer, which is depicted in Figure 6.18, is a first
specification towards a player who employs the strategy of moving their
tokens as fast as possible to the respective target fields. The idea behind
this strategy is to outrun other players by always moving the leading token.
In a case where the leading token cannot move, the token that has covered
the second biggest distance is moved, and so on. In order to implement
this strategy, two new rules moveFirst and moveFirstKO have to be specified.
In the control condition of the unit, these rules obviously have the highest
priority after the rules for moving out and freeing the start field, as can be
seen in Figure 6.18.

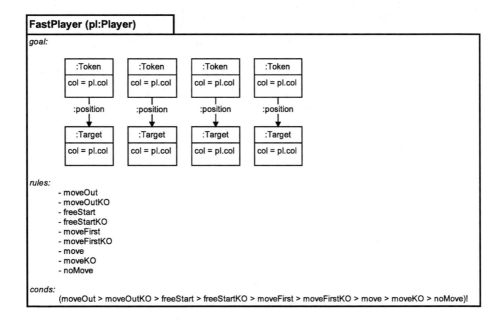

Figure 6.18: The FastPlayer unit

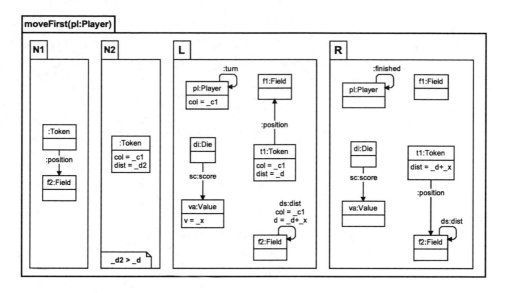

Figure 6.19: The rule moveFirst of the FastPlayer unit

The autonomous unit **FastPlayer** has the same goal as the previuosly introduced units **GentlePlayer** and **AggressivePlayer**. It also wants to move all of its tokens onto their respective target fields. The new rule **moveFirst** is depicted in Figure 6.19.

The left-hand side of this rule detects the following situation: it is the player's turn, the score of the die is _x, and a token of the player is located somewhere on the track. Furthermore, the destination field to which the token can move with the current score is determined. This is done analogously to the method in the previously described rules. This rule has two negative application conditions. The first one **N1** ensures that the rule is not applicable if any token is located at the destination field. The second NAC **N2** enforces the movement of the leading token. It demands that there is no token in the environment which has covered a bigger distance than the token determined by the left-hand side. Remember that the covered distance of a token is stored in the attribute **dist**. So this rule is only applicable if the token to be moved has the greatest attribute value **dist** of all tokens of the same color, i.e. if the token is in fact the leading one of its color.

If this rule is applied, the **turn** edge of the **Player** node is replaced by an edge of type **finished**, the **position** edge connecting t1 to f1 is deleted, and a new **position** edge is inserted, connecting t1 with f2. Furthermore, the distance of the token refered to by t1 is recalculated to the sum of the old distance plus the score of the die.

Analogously to the previously introduced movement rules, a variant with a knock out of a foreign token has to be provided. It is depicted in Figure 6.20.

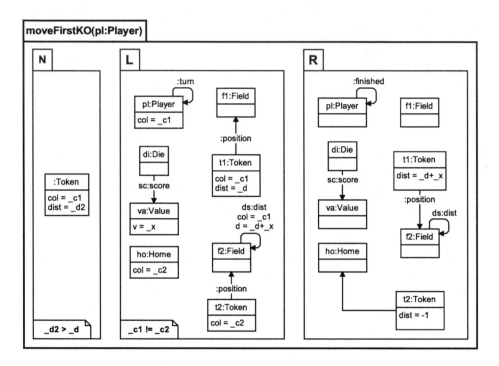

Figure 6.20: The rule moveFirstKO of the FastPlayer unit

It looks rather similar to the rule without knock out, except for the detection of a foreign token that is placed on the destination field. In order to perform the knock out, the home field of the foreign token is also determined. This rule has one NAC N which enforces the movement of the leading token in the same way as the NAC N2 of the rule moveFirst.

As mentioned earlier, this unit employs a strategy which is only a first step towards a true fast strategy. This is due to the fact that the leading token is considered only once in the control condition. Imagine the situation where a fast player has all their tokens on the track, the leading token is located directly in front of the target fields, and a score of 5 has been thrown. In this case, the leading token cannot move, so the rule moveFirst is not applicable. Neither is the rule moveFirstKO. In a true fast strategy the token that has covered the next most distance should be moved. But in the case of the autonomous unit specified here, a random token is now moved. One possibility to implement a true fast strategy would be to add two new rules moveSecond and moveSecondKO, which look very similar to the rules moveFirst, respectively moveFirstKO. In each of their left-hand sides the leading token is detected, i.e. a token which has covered a bigger distance than the one to be moved. The NAC is the same as in the rules moving the leading token. It then ensures that none of the remaining tokens have covered a bigger distance. These two rules would have to be integrated into the control condition with a priority just lower than the moveFirst rules, but higher than the ordinary move rules. Analogously, two rules with according priorities would have to be created for the token that has covered the third most distance, and integrated into the control condition.

6.4.6   The Autonomous Unit CompactPlayer

A fourth strategy that comes to mind regarding the game Ludo is to move the tokens in a compact way. Roughly speaking, the idea is that tokens in a close vicinity provide a certain amount of security in the sense that the leading tokens are protected by the trailing ones. It is dangerous for other players to knock out one of the leading tokens of such a group because they can in turn be knocked out by the trailing tokens of the group. The autonomous unit CompactPlayer, which is depicted in Figure 6.21, is a first specification towards a player who employs this strategy.

The idea is that moving the token on the track which has covered the smallest distance so far has the highest priority. If a player has more than one token out on the track, this strategy ensures that a group of tokens forms and moves in a compact way.

Analogously to the specification of the FastPlayer unit, two new rules moveLast and moveLastKO have to be specified. They are depicted in Figure 6.22 and Figure 6.23.

Both rules have a higher priority than the ordinary movement rules and are accordingly inserted into the control condition of the autonomous unit CompactPlayer. The rule moveLast is very similar to the rule moveFirst of the autonomous unit FastPlayer. The only difference is the application condition of the NAC. The NAC N2 together with its AC specifies that there is no token of the same color on the track ($\_d2 > -1$) which has covered a smaller distance than the selected token ($\_d2 < \_d$). The same is true for the rule moveLastKO.

The autonomous unit CompactPlayer is only a first step towards a player with a compact movement strategy. Moving the tokens in the most compact

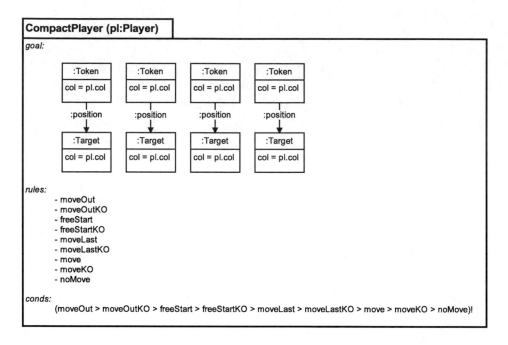

Figure 6.21: The CompactPlayer unit

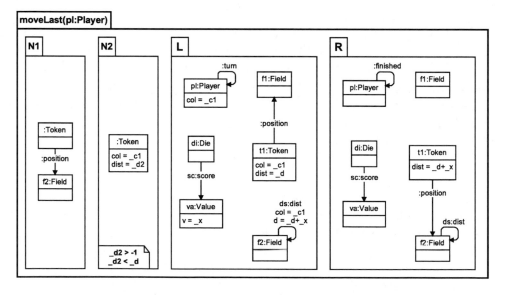

Figure 6.22: The rule moveLast of the CompactPlayer unit

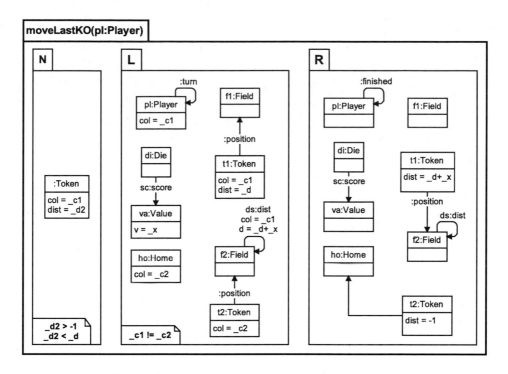

Figure 6.23: The rule moveLastKO of the CompactPlayer unit

possible way means to always move trailing tokens and never the leading one. But this is not always the case for the autonomous unit CompactPlayer. Consider a situation where the trailing token is blocked by a token of the same color. In this case, neither the rule moveLast (due to the NAC N1 which forbids any other token located at the destination field) nor the rule moveLastKO (in the left-hand side of which a foreign token located at the destination field is needed) is applicable. For this reason, the simple movement rules are tested next, yielding the selection of a random token for movement. This may be the wrong token, according to the perfect compact strategy. One way to solve this would be to add further rules for moving the second to last resp. the third to last token. These rules would then have a higher priority than the random movement rules.

6.5   Simulating Ludo with GrGen

A first implementation of the Ludo case study has been realized using the tool AGG [ERT99]. As stated earlier, AGG as well as GrGen provide a user interface that allows during run-time to specify a graph, to test whether a predefined rule matches (including AC and NAC), and to actually apply a rule to the graph. AGG allows for attribute value parameters in rules. So every player rule is specified once with a parameter for the color attribute. GrGen allows to parameterize rules with graph elements. Here every player rule is also specified once, but with the corresponding Player node as parameter.

An autonomous unit is implemented as an object that subsumes the necessary rules and stores the rule parameters. It also provides a method step, which tries to execute the next rule (using the interface of the underlying graph transformation engine) according to the control condition. This method does not rely on a general mechanism but is implemented manually for every control condition. If no rule is applicable, this method returns false, otherwise it applies the rule and returns true.

The community is represented by an object that subsumes all autonomous units and the environment graph. It also has a method step that executes the next step of the sequential community semantics by randomly choosing one of its autonomous units and asking it to apply a rule by invoking its step method. If this method returns false, meaning that a rule execution is not possible for this autonomous unit (e.g. if it is the turn of the blue player and a unit with a different color has been selected), another autonomous unit is randomly chosen. In order not to ask the same autonomous unit twice, the community keeps a list of those units that have already been asked in the current step. If a unit successfully applied a rule, the list is cleared and the step method of the community is invoked again. Should all units have been asked and neither of them been able to apply a rule, the derivation is assumed to be finished. Furthermore, it is checked after each step whether the overall goal of the community is reached. In the case of Ludo, this means that one player has placed all tokens on the respective target fields. This test is achieved by a graph transformation rule, in which the left-hand side, the common part, and the right-hand side are the same graph and specify the desired goal as a graph pattern. If the application of this rule succeeds, the derivation process is also considered to be finished.

Using AGG, the actual graph transformation can directly be observed using the GUI version of the tool. Figure 6.24 shows a screenshot of a Ludo game with the AGG visualization of the environment graph. Please note that the AGG specification differs from the specification presented here. For this reason, the environment graph does not look as expected.

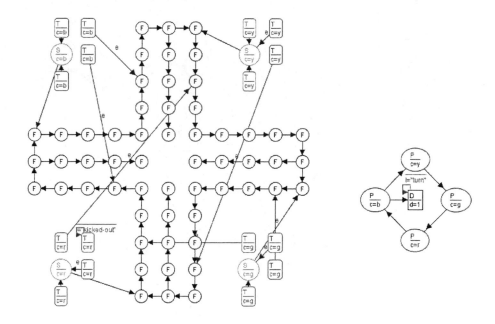

Figure 6.24: Screenshot of the Ludo graph in AGG

Since AGG as well as **GrGen** provide access to the current environment graph at any time, a generic visualization can be implemented in a straightforward way. Figure 6.25 shows an alternative, generic visualization of the situation depicted in Figure 6.24. This alternative visualization resembles the actual board game more closely. Since there are no restrictions to the generic visualization, the situation from the environment graph can even be visualized in a transport network as depicted in Figure 6.26.

The tool **GrGen** does not provide a direct visualization of the current environment graph (except for a textual description). For debugging purposes it is able to communicate with a commercial graph visualization tool that is part of the package. In the implementation used for the simulation of the Ludo specification presented here, a generic visualization has been implemented. A screenshot of a game situation can be seen in Figure 6.27.

In order to test for statistic differences in Ludo games with players employing different strategies, a significant number of games has to be simulated. It turned out that the AGG implementation was not suitable for these tests, since a single game took at least a few minutes (up to half an hour) even without drawing the graph in every step. The performance of **GrGen** is more adequate for these tests. Simulating a thousand games

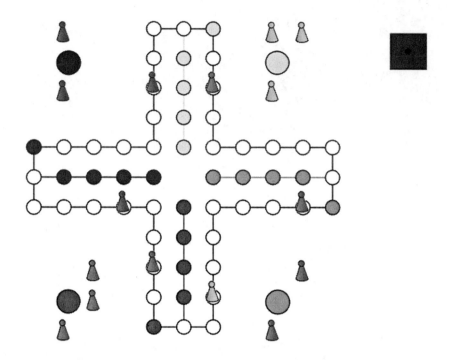

Figure 6.25: Screenshot of the generic Ludo graph in AGG

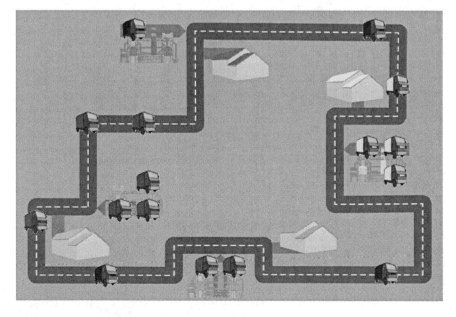

Figure 6.26: Screenshot of an alternative Ludo graph in AGG

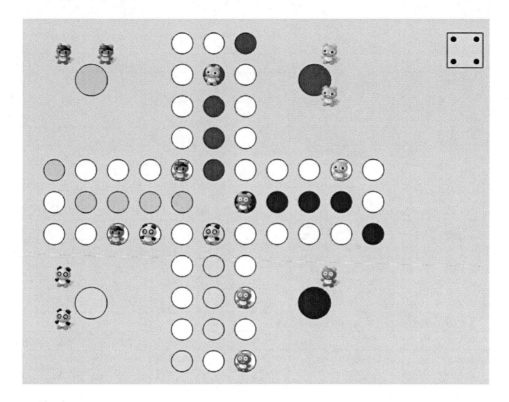

Figure 6.27: Screenshot of a generic graph visualization on top of **GrGen**

without drawing the graphs in intermediate steps takes well below a minute on the same machine. But even a simulation that includes the drawing of the current situation on the board after every step does not take longer than a few seconds. However, **GrGen** in its original implementation is not suitable for a graph transformation sytem that relies on a random selection of matches. A direct implementation of the specification discussed here will not yield the desired results in **GrGen** , since at least the rolling of the die as well as the selection of the starting player should happen in a random way. Asking the interface of **GrGen** for a match of a certain rule in the environment graph will always yield the same answer, i.e. the first match according to the deterministic match selection strategy of the tool. Especially for rolling the die this behavior is not desired. Luckily the interface of **GrGen** also provides access to the list of all matches of the rule under consideration. In the implementation used here, this list is taken and one match is then randomly selected, using a predefined **random** function of the .NET environment.

Community of gentle players							
	red		blue		yellow		green
wins	252		265		257		226
starts	254		238		269		239
start wins	64	[25,2%]	70	[29,4%]	76	[28,3%]	58 [24,3%]
Community of aggressive players							
	red		blue		yellow		green
wins	262		228		283		227
starts	255		250		242		253
start wins	73	[28,6%]	61	[24,4%]	68	[28,1%]	71 [28,1%]
Community of fast players							
	red		blue		yellow		green
wins	247		242		267		244
starts	252		242		240		266
start wins	61	[24,2%]	66	[27,3%]	62	[25,8%]	66 [24,8%]
Community of compact players							
	red		blue		yellow		green
wins	269		239		259		233
starts	258		244		241		257
start wins	74	[28,7%]	59	[24,2%]	72	[29,9%]	69 [26,8%]

Table 6.1: Results for communities with players using the same strategy

In the following a few results from the tests are presented. It is note-worthy that the results and implications are not to be taken seriously in a scientific way. They are merely intended as a proof of concept for the implementation of autonomous units.

The community used in the following simulations consists of players with the colors 'red', 'blue', 'yellow', and 'green', playing in that order. One simulation run consists of a thousand games of Ludo of the given community.

Table 6.1 shows the results for each community consisting of players with the same strategy.

The row 'wins' denotes the absolute number of games the according player won. The row 'starts' shows the number of games in which the corresponding player started the game. Finally the row 'start wins' denotes the games in which the corresponding player started and won together with a percentage compared to the number of games in which the player started.

	red(aggr)	blue(fast)	yellow(comp)	green(gentle)
wins	386	348	114	152
starts	259	234	257	250
start wins	94 [36,3%]	84 [35,9%]	29 [11,3%]	33 [13,2%]

Table 6.2: Results for a community with every strategy

This result is used to determine whether a player who starts a game has a higher or lower chance of winning the game.

The number of starts for each color is almost equally distributed except for random fluctuations. This is an expected result, since the die randomly decides the starting player and this is independent of any employed player strategy. The number of wins for each color is also almost equally distributed, which again is an expected result. Since every player employs the same strategy in each simulation run, the winner should be determined by pure chance. The starting player also has no significant higher or lower chance to win the game, since every player wins about twenty-four to twenty-nine percent of the games they started. This can be considered a random fluctuation.

In order to determine whether one strategy has a significant winning chance over another, the next simulation run was executed in a mixed community with every strategy involved. The results are shown in Table 6.2. Here the red player plays aggressively, green employs the gentle strategy, blue the fast strategy, and yellow plays in a compact way.

Here is a significant result. The players employing the fast and aggressive strategies win over seventy percent of the games. Playing in a compact style seems to be the weakest strategy in a completely mixed community. The aggressive and fast strategies seem to have an advantage in starting the game, but actually the start win ratios almost perfectly reflect the overall win game situation. A player who wins p percent of overall games, also wins about p percent of the games which the same player started.

In order to determine the weakest strategy, the next simulation run was executed with a community in which the blue player employed the compact strategy, while the other players used the gentle method. The results are depicted in Table 6.3.

In fact the player using the compact strategy wins the fewest games, but not in a truly significant way. The results are almost equally distributed, as is the start win percentage that again reflects the overall win situation. So

	red		blue(compact)		yellow		green	
wins	246		234		280		240	
starts	247		227		260		266	
start wins	57	[23,1%]	52	[22,9%]	75	[28,8%]	65	[24,4%]

Table 6.3: Results for a community with compact and gentle strategies

	red		blue		yellow		green(gentle)	
wins	241		251		211		297	
starts	247		244		254		255	
start wins	64	[25,9%]	60	[24,6%]	56	[22%]	74	[29%]

Table 6.4: Results for a community with gentle and compact strategies

	red(aggr)		blue		yellow		green	
wins	231		239		269		261	
starts	252		238		234		276	
start wins	55	[21,8%]	57	[24%]	64	[27,4%]	78	[28,3%]

Table 6.5: Results for a community with aggressive and fast strategies

the next simulation run was done the other way round, with a community consisting of one player using the gentle strategy while the other players employed the compact strategy. Table 6.4 shows the results.

This result seems to prove that the gentle strategy is slighty better than the compact strategy. Even a single player employing the gentle strategy wins the most games in a community with otherwise compact players. The start win percentage does again show no conspicuous results.

In order to determine the best strategy, the next simulation run was executed in a community where the red player employed the aggressive strategy while the others used the fast strategy. Table 6.5 shows the results.

Although the player with the aggressive strategy wins the fewest games in this run, the overall wins are almost equally distributed. So the next simulation run is done the other way round, with only one player using the fast strategy while the other players use the aggressive style. Table 6.6 shows the results.

The player with the fast strategy wins the most games, but not in a

	red	blue(fast)	yellow	green
wins	243	285	255	217
starts	239	266	249	246
start wins	55 [23%]	76 [28,6%]	69 [27,7%]	54 [22%]

Table 6.6: Results for a community with fast and aggressive strategies

	red	blue	yellow	green(fast)
wins	172	171	178	479
starts	252	240	266	242
start wins	49 [19,4%]	173 [17,3%]	43 [16,2%]	121 [50%]

Table 6.7: Results for a community with fast and compact strategies

	red	blue	yellow	green(fast)
wins	188	173	477	162
starts	262	242	252	244
start wins	49 [18,7%]	43 [17,8%]	105 [41,7%]	37 [15,2%]

Table 6.8: Results for a community with aggressive and compact strategies

significant way. This result may again be caused by random fluctuations. So it is not clear which of the two strategies is truly the better one, but the assumption from the first mixed community simulation run has not been disproved either. In order to see whether one of these strategies is really superior to the statistically weakest strategy, the next simulation done was executed in a community with one fast player against three compact players. Table 6.7 shows the results.

In this simulation run the result is very clear. The only player using the fast strategy wins almost half of the games. So the fast strategy definitely seems to be the better strategy, at least against players using the compact strategy. But the same is true for the aggressive strategy as can be seen in Table 6.8.

Whether or not these simulation runs seem suitable to determine the best or the weakest strategy for the game Ludo, the simulation results clearly show two things. First of all the implementation of the random match selection is sufficient, as can be seen by the fact that there is an almost equal distribution of the starting players over all tables. The red player started 25,4% of the games, the blue player 24,2%, yellow 25,1%, and green 25,4%. The second fact is, that besides random fluctuations the result of the games is significantly influenced by players using different strategies.

6.6   Concluding Remark

In this chapter a case study has been presented in which the board game Ludo has been modeled by a community of autonomous units. Here every player as well as the die are modeled as an autonomous unit. The used control conditions are based on priorities and determine the way the participants play the game. Four different strategies have been presented, starting with a gentle player who only kicks out another player's token when there is no other way. The opposite strategy has also been modeled, i.e. a player who kicks out other player's token whenever this is possible. A player strategy in which the leading token is moved whenever modeled has also been modeled. The idea is to reach the target fields as fast as possible. A preliminary realization of the opposite strategy, in which a player tries to move the tokens in the most compact way, has also been presented. It is preliminary because an arbitrary token is moved if the last one is blocked. For a true compact strategy the tokens should be moved in the order from last to first. The same is true for the fast strategy. If the leading token is blocked, an arbitrary token is moved. For a true fast strategy the tokens should be moved in the order from first to last.

Nevertheless, the specifications presented in this chapter show that autonomous units can be used in a straightforward way to model autonomous participants of a board game even employing different ways to play the game and reach their individual goal.

Chapter 7

Case Study: Ants

In Chapter 3 a very basic model of a colony of foraging ants has been introduced. The ant colony has been modeled as a community of autonomous units, each of which represents an ant. In this chapter, a more sophisticated model of foraging ants is introduced and discussed, employing the concept of a community of autonomous units in the same way.

7.1 Ant Colony Optimization

As explained in [BDT99], many ant species have trail-laying trail-following behavior when foraging. At first, ants randomly choose a path in order to find a food source. While they walk, they leave a trail of a chemical substance called *pheromone*. Now succeeding foraging ants are stimulated to follow a path with the highest concentration of pheromones with a high probability. In [DAGP90] a model of these probabilistic values has been developed, which closely matches the experimental observations. In the experiment, a bridge with two different but equally long bridges connect the anthill with the food source. As long as there is no pheromone on either of the bridges, foragers randomly select one of them. Although this selection is purely random, fluctuations occur, leading to a slightly higher amount of foragers choosing one bridge over the other. This leads to a slightly higher concentration of pheromone on that bridge, which in turn stimulates more succeeding foragers to choose that bridge, and so on. Here pheromone evaporation is not considered, since the experiments typically last shorter than the evaporation rate of pheromones.

In [GADP89], the experiment above is extended, employing two bridges of different lengths. Again the amplification of initial random fluctuations yields the selection of the shortest path in most cases. But in some cases, the longer bridge is chosen and then amplified. Moreover, this strategy does not allow for the adaptation to a changed environment situation, as another experiment shows. Here the food source and the anthill are initially only connected by the longer bridge, forcing the foraging ants to choose it. After thirty minutes, the amplification of the initial selection is already so high that the foragers do not select the new, much shorter path to the food source. This shows that a foraging strategy based on pheromones only is not very flexible.

The ant species *Lasius Niger* also utilizes a pheromone following strategy but additionally employs individual ant memory. If foragers of this species detect that they head almost perpendicularly to the direction of the anthill or the already visited food source, they turn back [BDG92] and choose a different route. This combination of individual memory and collective trail following turns out to be more flexible, as the same experiment as above shows. Here ants of this species prove more flexible, since they manage to select the shorter path after some time.

With these results of the biological experiments, the problem of finding the shortest path between two locations can be approached. It is the emergent result of a number of ants to find a shortest path between two locations, so a model which takes into account the experimental findings can be useful. Modeling a single ant as an autonomous unit may yield a community that finds a shortest path between an anthill and a food source, and that may even be sufficiently flexible to adapt to a new situation.

The basic idea underlying the ant colony optimization algorithms is to use positive feedback ([DMC91, DMC96]) analogously to the pheromone trail following behavior. A virtual pheromone that is used as an amplifier allows for the memorization of good solutions, from which even better solutions can be made up. In order to avoid stagnation of the algorithm, negative feedback is used in the form of pheromone evaporation.

In the following section, a community of autonomous units is presented, which models an ant colony that utilizes pheromone trail following together with a basic form of individual memory. This model is realized as a generic implementation using the graph transformation engine of **GrGen** , analogously to the implementation of the game Ludo in Chapter 6.

7.2 Ant Graph Model

In this section, the type graph of the underlying graphs of the ant colony model is introduced. It is depicted in Figure 7.1.

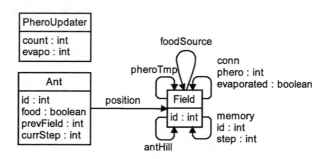

Figure 7.1: The type graph of the ant community

The node type **Field** represents a field on which ants can be located and has an integer attribute **id**, which stores the unique identifier of the field. The anthill and the food source are special fields, indicated by corresponding loop edges of type **antHill** resp. **foodSource**. Fields are interconnected by edges of type **conn** in both directions, representing paths between ant locations. An integer attribute **phero** stores the current pheromone concentration of the path. Ants leave pheromones only on their way back from the food source to the nest. Due to the fact that evaporation of pheromones is modeled here as well, an additional Boolean attribute **evaporated** is needed for technical reasons and explained later.

In this model, an ant is represented by a node of type **Ant**. Its unique identifier is stored in the integer attribute **id**. Whether the ant is carrying food or not is indicated by the Boolean attribute **food**. Since ants should not directly walk back to a location they visited in the directly previous step, the integer attribute **prevField** stores the identifier of the **Field** node the ant has just come from. The integer attribute **currStep** is used for the tracking back to the nest using the memorized path and is explained further below. The location of an ant is represented by an edge of type **position** that connects an **Ant** node with the corresponding **Field** node.

Ants are modeled here in such a way that they memorize the path from their nest to the food source. Once they discover food, they pick it up and follow the memorized path back to the anthill. Since there is no internal memory concept for autonomous units, this information has to be stored in the common environment. This is done by edges of type memory that connect the respective fields in the direction of the actual ant movement. In order to assign these memory edges to their rightful owner, an integer attribute id is used which has the same value as the corresponding id attribute of the respective ant. On tracking the memorized path back, these memory edges are deleted since the memory is rebuilt on every way from nest to food source.

Please note that the memorized path may comprise circles. Imagine an ant that walks along the fields 1, 2, 3, and 4, from there back to field 2, and then to field 5, and further to the food source. Now tracking back the memorized path, the ant will at some point be located at field 2, coming from field 5. Now it has two edges of type memory to choose from, the one connecting the fields 4 and 2, and the one connecting the fields 1 and 2. If it chooses the latter, the edge connecting fields 2 and 3 and the edge connecting fields 4 and 2 remain in the environment. They may interfere with future path memorization, so a feature must be added to the model which forces the ant to walk back the precise way it memorized including circles. For this reason, the memory edge has an integer attribute step, which stores the walking step in which the edge has been created. The current walking step is stored in the attribute currStep of the ant. On the way from the nest to the food source, this attribute value is increased with every step, and on the way back from the food source it is decreased with every step. Thus it allows to track back the precise route the ant originally took.

In this model, the ants are intended to walk in parallel in every step. For this reason, it is not possible for one ant to directly increase the pheromone level of a connecting edge, as this would result in a conflict in case two ants carrying food walk along the same edge. For this reason, a parallel edge of type pheroTmp is used, which is inserted into the environment by ants while carrying food. This mechanism avoids conflicts in accessing and changing the pheromone levels of the conn edges. In order to update the pheromone levels of the conn edges, an autonomous unit with a special rule will be used. This autonomous unit also handles the evaporation of the pheromones and manifests itself as a node of type PheroUpdater. Its integer attribute count counts the derivation steps. If a step count is reached that equals the value of the attribute evapo, the evaporation takes place and the counter is reset to 0. The amount of pheromone units that will vanish in one evaporation step is determined by the value of the attribute amount. For this reason, the attributes evapo and amount should be set to suitable values in the initial environment.

7.3 The Ant Community

The community that models the ant colony mainly consists of autonomous units for every ant of the colony. Besides these units, two special autonomous units are needed for the updating of the pheromone levels of the field connecting edges and for the evaporation of pheromones. The following sections present the specifications of these autonomous units.

7.3.1 The Autonomous Unit **Ant**

Every ant of the ant colony is modeled by an autonomous unit that comprises rules for the ant movement. Initially, an ant is located at the anthill and starts foraging. This situation is addressed by the rule **forage** that is depicted in Figure 7.2.

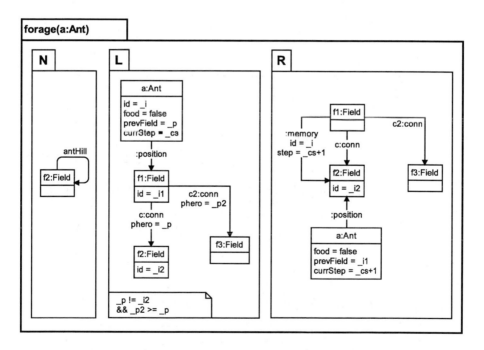

Figure 7.2: The rule forage

The parameter of the rule is a placeholder for the actual ant node **a**. The left-hand side of this rule detects a situation where the ant is located at the field f1 and carries no food. The field f1 is connected to at least two fields f2 resp. f3. The NAC N demands that the field f2 is not marked as the anthill. The application condition ensures that the id of the field f2 is different from the prevID attribute value of the ant node and that the pheromone level of the edge c is lower or equal to that of edge c2. When this rule is applied, the ant is moved to the field f2 which results in the replacement of the original position edge with a new position edge connecting the ant with the field f2. The prevField attribute value is set to the value of the id attribute value of the field f1 on which the ant was originally located. The step counter currStep of the ant is increased by one. In order to memorize the walking step, an edge of type memory is inserted with its id attribute value set to the id of the ant and the step attribute value to the original step of the ant plus one. Please note that this rule purposefully chooses a path that has a lower pheromone level than another path, i.e. it never chooses the path leaving the current field with the highest pheromone level.

The rule followPhero, which handles a foraging ant that follows the pheromone trail is depicted in Figure 7.3.

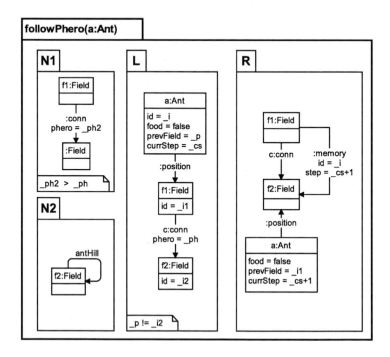

Figure 7.3: The rule followPhero

Again, its parameter **a** references the actual ant node. Its left-hand side detects a situation where the ant is carrying no food and is located at the field **f1** which is connected to the field **f2** by the edge **c**. The application condition ensures that the field **f2** is not the field on which the ant was located in the directly previous step. The NAC **N1** demands that the field **f1** is not connected to any other field by a **conn** edge with a higher pheromone level than **c**. The NAC **N2** ensures that the field **f2** is not the anthill since it makes no sense to walk back there without any food. Analogously to the rule **forage**, the application of this rule yields the movement of the ant to the field **f2** and the insertion of a corresponding memory edge.

The rule **forage** is only applicable if at least two **conn** edges leave the field on which the ant is currently located while the **followPhero** is only applicable if the destination field is different from the field the ant was located on in the directly previous step. Imagine a field being a dead end, i.e. a field that is only connected to one other field. If an ant is located on such a field, the two rules above are not applicable (and will never be), so that the ant would be stuck. For this reason, a simple rule **walk** is also part of the model, which ignores all constraints and simply walks along one path. It is depicted in Figure 7.4.

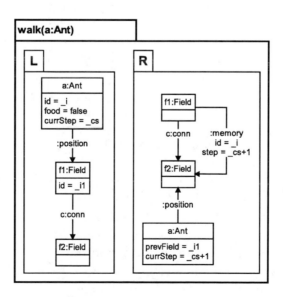

Figure 7.4: The rule **walk**

Its parameter **a** again references the actual ant node. The rule is applicable if the ant carries no food and is located at a field f1 which is connected to a field f2. The application of this rule yields the movement of the ant to the field f2. Analogously to the rules forage and followPhero, the position edge is replaced accordingly and a memory edge is inserted.

Using the three rules introduced so far, an ant can already walk along an area of interconnected fields. It will even enter a field that is marked as a food source, but so far it will not recognize it. For this reason, the rule walkToFood, which is depicted in Figure 7.5, is specified.

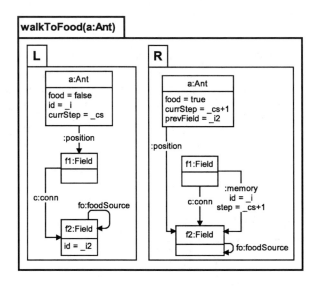

Figure 7.5: The rule walkToFood

Its parameter a again references the actual ant node. The rule is applicable if the ant carries no food and is located at a field f1 which is connected to a field f2 marked as food source by a loop edge of type foodSource. The application of this rule yields a movement of the ant to the food source. Since the ant picks up some food, its attribute value food is set to true. Analogously to the rules above, the current step counter currStep is updated and a corresponding memory edge is inserted.

Now that the ant has found food, it heads back to the nest, following its memorized path and depositing pheromones on the way. The rule walkWithFood, depicted in Figure 7.6, handles this.

Its parameter a again references the actual ant node. The rule is applicable if the ant carries food and is located at a field f1. Additionally, a memory edge belonging to the ant (indicated by equal id values) with an at-

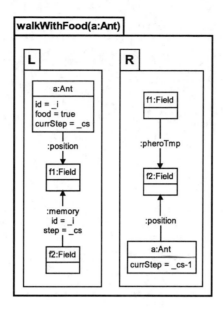

Figure 7.6: The rule walkWithFood

tribute value **step** equaling the attribute value **currStep** of the ant connects
another field **f2** with **f1**. The application of this rule yields a movement
of the ant to the field **f2** by replacing the **position** edge accordingly. The
memory edge is deleted and the **currStep** counter of the ant is decreased.
Furthermore, the pheromone deposit is represented by the corresponding
insertion of an edge of type **pheroTmp**.

This rule may also be applied in the last step of the way back to the nest,
since there is no constraint prohibiting the ant from entering the anthill.
The way back to the anthill is handled by a special rule **walkToHill** that is
depicted in Figure 7.7. As can be seen later, this rule has a higher priority
than the rule **walkWithFood**, so that rule can actually not be applied in the
last step on the way back to the nest.

The parameter **a** of the rule again references the actual ant node. The
rule is applicable in a situation that is similar to that for the rule **walkWith-
Food**, except that the field **f2** has to be marked as anthill by a loop edge
of type **antHill**. The application of this rule yields a movement of the ant
to the anthill by replacing the **position** edge accordingly. The **memory** edge
is deleted, a **pheroTmp** is inserted, the **currStep** counter of the ant is set
to 0, and the food is dropped by setting the attribute value **food** to **false**.
Furthermore, the previous field **prevField** is set to the **id** of anthill field **f2**.

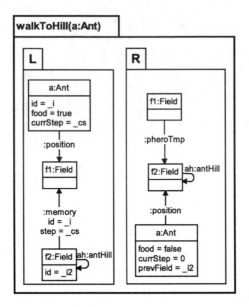

Figure 7.7: The rule walkToHill

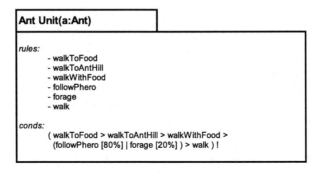

Figure 7.8: The autonomous unit representing an ant

The six rules presented so far complete the rule set for the autonomous unit **Ant Unit** which is depicted in Figure 7.8.

The **Ant Unit** has no explicit goal, which means that it allows every environment as a goal. The rules that have been introduced earlier are all part of an **Ant Unit**, but they may not be applied freely. The control condition imposes the following restriction on the rule application process. First of all, the subcondition in brackets is applied as long as possible. This subcondition yields a single rule application by specifying different priorities for the contained rules, as indicated by the operator '>'. Only one of the six rules is allowed to be applied in every derivation step, depending on their priorities. If the leftmost rule is applicable, then it has to be applied, completing the subcondition. Only if it is not applicable, the rules denoted further to the right may be applied. This means that the application of the rule walkWithFood is only allowed by the subcondition if the rules walkToFood and walkToHill are both not applicable. If the rule walkWithFood is also not applicable, the subcondition in brackets is evaluated. The operator '—' specifies a choice, i.e. one of the rules separated by the operator is chosen to be applied. The rules forage and followPhero are specified in such a way that they are both applicable in a given situation. The percentage value specifies the probability of the selection of the respective rule, i.e. there is a probability of 4:1 that the rule followPhero is chosen. Only if all other rules are not applicable, the rule walk is applied. This is a safeguard for environment graphs with dead ends. This rule is not needed if the environment graph is guaranteed to have at least two neighbors for every field.

7.3.2 The Autonomous Unit **PheroUpdater**

So far the application of any rule of an Ant Unit does not update the pheromone level of a conn edge. But in order for the ant rules to work in the intended way the correct pheromone level has to be set. For this reason, a very simple autonomous unit with the name PheroUpdater Unit is specified, which comprises the rules updatePhero, noEvaporate and evaporate. This autonomous unit manifests itself in the environment as a node of type PheroUpdater. The rule updatePhero is depicted in Figure 7.9.

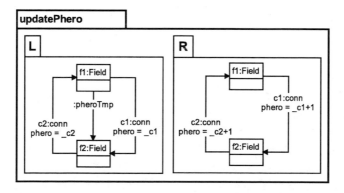

Figure 7.9: The rule updatePhero

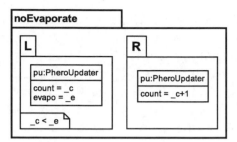

Figure 7.10: The rule noEvaporate

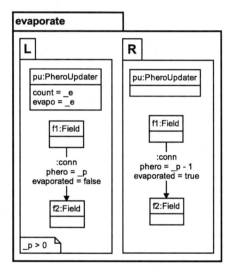

Figure 7.11: The rule evaporate

It is used to delete every edge of type **pheroTmp** and to increase the pheromone levels on the corresponding **conn** edges with every deletion.

The rule **noEvaporate**, depicted in Figure 7.10, is applicable whenever the value of the step counter **count** of the **PheroUpdater** node is below the value of the attribute **evapo**. The application of this rule simply increases the counter.

The rule **evaporate** is depicted in Figure 7.11. This rule is applicable if the step counter **count** of the **PheroUpdater** node equals the value of its attribute **evapo**. In this case, a **conn** edge connecting two fields is determined that has not yet been used in this evaporation process (indicated by the

value false of the evaporated attribute) and that has a phero value greater
0. Applying the rule yields the evaporation of pheromone by decreasing
the phero attribute of the corresponding edge, according to the value of
the attribute amount of the PheroUpdater node. In order to prevent further
evaporation in the same process, the evaporated value is set to true.

In order to prepare the next evaporation step, the evaporated attribute
values of the conn edges have to be set to false again. This is done by the rule
resetEvaporated, which is so simple that it is omitted here. Furthermore, a
rule resetCounter to reset the step counter count of the PheromoneUpdater
node is needed. This rule is applicable if the value of the count attribute
equals the value of the attribute evapo and by applying the rule, the counter
is set to 0. The actual rule specification is omitted here, since it looks very
similar to the rule noEvaporate.

The autonomous unit PheroUpdater Unit is depicted in Figure 7.12. It
has no explicit goal, which means that it allows every environment as a goal.
It comprises the rules explained earlier. Its control condition specifies that
first the rule updatePhero has to be applied as long as possible. This will
result in the removal of all edges of type pheroTmp and the according update
of the phero attribute values of the conn edges. If the respective step for
an evaporation is not reached yet, the rule noEvaporate is applicable and
therefore applied, finishing the control condition. If the evaporation step is
reached, the subcondition in brackets is executed. Then the rule evaporate
will be applied as long as possible, meaning that all pheromone values of the
conn edges are reduced once. After that the rule resetEvaporated is applied
also as long as possible, in order to reset the evaporated attribute values of
every conn edge for a later evaporation step. Finally the rule resetCounter
is applied, which resets the step counter of the PheroUpdater node.

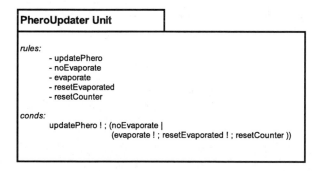

Figure 7.12: The autonomous unit PheroUpdater Unit

Now all the ingredients for the simulation of a foraging ant colony have been presented. In order to simulate a foraging ant colony, a community of autonomous units is used, which comprises an **Ant Unit** for every ant of the colony. Additionally one **PheroUpdater Unit** is part of the community.

The process to be investigated here consists of a parallel step of all **Ant Units** participating in the community, followed by a sequential execution of the complete control condition of the **PheroUpdater Unit**. Formally this can be achieved by a further autonomous unit which imports all the other units and employs a suitable control condition.

7.4   Simulating an Ant Community with GrGen

The tool **GrGen** is not yet capable of a parallel rule application as desired in this case study. For this reason, the implementation is realized with a suitable sequential rule application which is equivalent to a parallel rule application of all ants. Obviously, no rule application of an **Ant Unit** changes the environment in a way that influences other **Ant Units**. The decision whether or not to follow a pheromone trail is made independently of the current state of the environment graph. If an ant decides to follow the pheromone trail, it reads the pheromone level of the respective **conn** edges, which is not updated by any ant movement. For this reason, the implementation is realized with a scheduler that initiates exactly one rule for every ant. After every **Ant Unit** has applied exactly one rule according to its control condition, the control condition of the **PheroUpdater** unit is executed completely. These rule applications form one step in the simulation, i.e. one step comprises the movement of every ant together with evaporation and updates of the pheromone levels.

In order to test whether a small colony already finds a shortest path between its nest and a food source, an environment as depicted in Figure 7.13 is used. The figure actually shows a screenshot of the generic visualization of the implementation. As can be seen, the colony consists of ten ants, initially located at the anthill in the lower left. The shortest path to the food source in the upper right is obviously the diagonal connection. In a first simulation run the evaporation rate is set to take place every ten steps with the amount of one.

Usually, a situation as depicted in Figure 7.14 develops after about five thousand steps. Here the shortest path along the diagonal connections is the one with the highest pheromone concentration, at least in relation to the starting point and the actual shortest path. As the Figure shows, the diago-

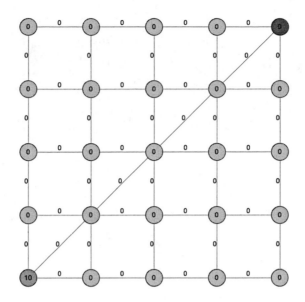

Figure 7.13: The initial environment of the ant colony

nal connection leaving the anthill has the highest pheromone concentration
of all leaving connections, so an ant usually chooses that connection. For
the second connection the same is true. Here the diagonal connection also
has the highest pheromone concentration of all leaving connections (except
for the one leading back to the anthill, but that connection is never chosen
due to the previous field checking mechanism of the rules). The same is
true for the third and the fourth diagonal connection, so in the terms of
the considered model the colony managed to find the shortest path.

But while the pheromone level of the first resp. the fourth diagonal
connection is significantly high compared to the alternative connections,
this is not the case for the second and third diagonal connection. Here
the pheromone levels are only slightly higher than those of the alternative
connections. This situation even turns out to be instable, i.e. a few steps
earlier or later the pheromone level of an alternative connection is higher
than that of the diagonal connection. Even for a much larger amount of
steps the situation will not become stable. So the colony with the given
setup does only find and mark the shortest path in intermediate steps, and
marks a longer path in other intermediate steps.

In order to see whether this effect arises from the fact that the colony

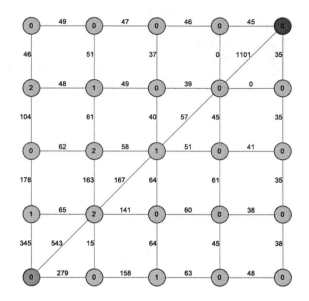

Figure 7.14: The environment of the ant colony after about 5000 steps

might comprise too few ants, another simulation with fifty ants and otherwise the same setup is tested. It turns out that the result is even more instable, since only the last diagonal connection leading towards the food source has a significantly high pheromone level. In simulation runs with this setup, even the first diagonal connection has lower pheromone levels than alternative connections in intermediate steps.

The next change in the setup affects the amount of pheromone evaporation. The simulation is run with a colony of ten ants again, with evaporation after ten steps but with the amount of two. This yields roughly the same effect as in the same setup with an evaporation amount of one. Only the situation for the second and third diagonal connection becomes more unstable, i.e. the respective diagonal connection is marked with a lower pheromone level than the alternative connections more often. Also, the pheromone level on the first diagonal connection stays only slightly higher than those of the alternative connections leading away from the anthill.

For this reason, further simulation runs have been executed with a shorter pheromone lifespan. The setup contains ten ants and the pheromone level is reduced by one after eight steps. In this case, the colony is rather successful. Figure 7.15 shows the environment after five thousand steps.

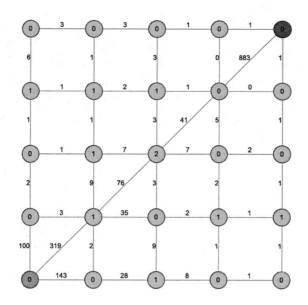

Figure 7.15: The environment of the ant colony after about 5000 steps

Although the amount of pheromones on the second resp. third diagonal connection is still not very high, it is about two times higher than the pheromone levels of the according alternative connections. Even more interesting is the fact that it stays that way even after a much higher amount of steps. So this setup can be considered stable.

Further reduction of the pheromone's lifespan yields no improvement. Simulation runs with a colony of ten ants and pheromone evaporation after seven steps with the amount one seem to be slightly instable. Most of the time, the correct shortest path is marked, but there are a few intermediate steps in which the second resp. third diagonal connection is marked with a lower pheromone level than the alternative connections. This effect worsens for an evaporation after six steps. If the evaporation takes place after five steps, or even more often, the shortest path marking becomes highly unstable. The absolute pheromone levels on the second and third diagonal connection then become rather small (below five) and only seldom exceed the pheromone levels of the alternative connections.

7.5   Concluding Remark

In this chapter, a case study has been presented in which a colony of foraging ants is modeled by a community of autonomous units. Here every ant as well as an evaporator is modeled as an autonomous unit. The used control conditions of the ant units are based on priorities and probabilistic choice. Every ant memorizes the way from the anthill to the food source by inserting respective edges into the environment. Once an ant detects a food source, it picks up some food and follows its memorized trail back to the nest, depositing one unit of pheromone on every part of the trail. On the way back the memorized trail is erased, i.e. the ant has completely forgotten about the trail once it arrives back at the anthill. After delivering the food, the ant leaves the nest and starts to search for food again. In every step the ant follows the path with the highest pheromone concentration with a probability of eighty percent and a random path with a probability of twenty percent. After a certain number of steps, some of the pheromone deposited on the path evaporates. The number of steps and the amount of evaporated pheromone can be adjusted in the beginning.

The ant colony has been implemented using the tool **GrGen** and a few simulation runs have been executed. The results show that even a small colony of ten ants finds a shortest path in a suitable setting. The simulation results also show that changes in the parameters, like a more frequent evaporation or a higher pheromone evaporation amount influence the results, yielding an instable shortest path marking or even circumventing the detection of a shortest path in general.

Chapter 8

Conceptional Background

In this chapter, some fundamental aspects of the semantics of rule-based systems are sketched and related to the semantics of visual models, as presented in [KHK06]. A rule-based system comprises a set of rules and some control conditions including descriptions of initial and terminal configurations. Semantically, the rules specify a binary relation on configurations of some kind by means of rule applications which are restricted according to the control conditions. As visual models are usually represented by diagrams, graphs or similar configurations, the rule-based setting can be employed to provide visual models with semantics.

Traditional programs and specifications are represented as textual expressions and strings with some grammatical structure. Their semantics is often operationally defined by term rewriting or state transition or denotationally given as a mapping into a semantic domain that reflects the syntactic structure. In recent years, visual models have become very popular in systems development in addition to textual descriptions as the widespread use of UML and Petri nets proves. Visual models are syntactically represented by diagrams, graphs, or similar configurations of some kind. Although they are intentionally more intuitive and suggestive than textual descriptions, their meaning must be fixed to avoid misunderstandings and mistakes. Like in the case of text-based modeling languages, there are the two possibilities of operational and denotational semantics even in the case of visual models in principle. In contrast to the textual case, the semantics of visual models is not yet worked out systematically, but a number of tentative proposals can be found in the literature. Many of them point in the direction that the transformation of graphs, diagrams, or other kinds of configurations may play a similar central role as term rewriting in the traditional case of textual models. In this chapter, the semantic potentials of a rule-based setting as it is provided by e.g. the area of graph transformation is sketched.

8.1   Rules and their Application

The objective of rules is their application to some kind of configuration like strings, terms, graphs, diagrams, pictures, etc. The application of a rule to a configuration derives a configuration. By means of all of its applications, a rule as a syntactic item yields a binary relation on configurations as a basic semantic entity.

The elementary ingredients of a rule-based setting are a set $\mathcal{K}$ of *configurations*, a set $\mathcal{R}$ of *rules*, and a *rule application operator* $\Longrightarrow$ that assigns a binary relation $\underset{r}{\Longrightarrow} \subseteq \mathcal{K} \times \mathcal{K}$ to each rule $r \in \mathcal{R}$.

A rule application $con \underset{r}{\Longrightarrow} con'$ is called direct derivation, derivation step, computation step, transition step, evaluation step, or something like this depending on the framework the rules are used in.

Since the semantic relations of rules are binary relations on configurations, set theoretic operations like the union, the sequential composition, etc. are acquired for free. In particular, the union $\underset{P}{\Longrightarrow} = \underset{r \in P}{\bigcup} \underset{r}{\Longrightarrow}$ for a set $P \in \mathcal{R}$ of rules and the reflexive and transitive closure $\underset{P}{\overset{*}{\Longrightarrow}}$ of $\underset{P}{\Longrightarrow}$ are obtained.

This allows one to consider a set $P \subseteq \mathcal{R}$ of rules as the most elementary version of a rule-based system with two variants of semantics.

1. **Rule application graph:** $Graph(P) = (\mathcal{K}, \underset{P}{\Longrightarrow})$ with the configurations as nodes and the rule applications as edges.

2. **Iterated rule application relation:** $\underset{P}{\overset{*}{\Longrightarrow}} \subseteq \mathcal{K} \times \mathcal{K}$.

$Graph(P)$ is a proper operational semantics while $\underset{P}{\overset{*}{\Longrightarrow}}$ only indicates what is reachable from which configuration and abstracts from the intermediate configurations. In grammatical frameworks, $Graph(P)$ is known as the derivation graph and $\underset{P}{\overset{*}{\Longrightarrow}}$ as the derivation relation. In the area of Petri nets, $Graph(P)$ is the reachability graph and $\underset{P}{\overset{*}{\Longrightarrow}}$ the usual firing relation.

Example

As a running example, well-structured flow diagrams (see, e.g., Farrow, Kennedy, and Zucconi [FKZ76]) are discussed, which are well-known visual models and quite typical predecessors of more modern diagrams like the UML diagrams.

A well-structured flow diagram has a unique entry (depicted as a small circle) and a unique exit (depicted as a small square) and is composed of basic statements and decisions indicated by boxes resp. diamonds (cf. Figure 8.1). A diamond is inscribed with a Boolean expression. A basic statement may have an empty box or a box inscribed with an assignment statement. The empty box represents a nonterminal placeholder for another well-structured flow diagram. The first three rules in Figure 8.1 show that such a placeholder may be replaced by an assignment, a compound statement, or a *while*-loop. The control flow in the well-structured flow diagram is given by the direction of the edges. While the exit is never the source of further control flow, every other node is followed by a unique basic statement or decision. The two edges leaving a decision diamond are labeled with T (for true) resp. F (for false), indicating that the direction of the control flow depends on the evaluation of the Boolean expression. Moreover, we assume the natural numbers $\mathbb{N}$ as the only data type and k variables $X_1, \ldots, X_k$ for some $k \in \mathbb{N}$. Then the textual rules in Figure 8.1 specify that the available arithmetic expressions (to be assigned to a variable) are 0, successor or predecessor of a variable and that the inequality predicate of two variables is the only Boolean expression.

rules :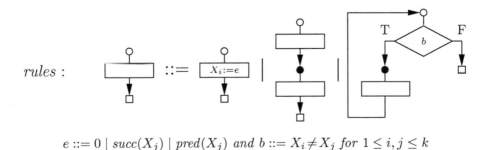

$$e ::= 0 \mid succ(X_j) \mid pred(X_j) \ and \ b ::= X_i \neq X_j \ for \ 1 \leq i, j \leq k$$

Figure 8.1: Rules to refine well-structured flow diagrams

Altogether, the rules describe all possible refinements of well-structured flow diagrams. Figure 8.2 shows a sample derivation which refines a com-

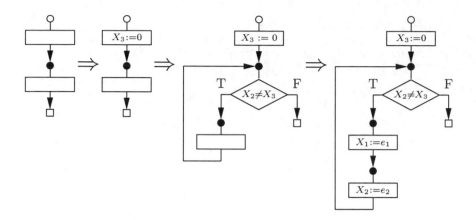

Figure 8.2: An example of a derivation sequence

pound statement with two nonterminal boxes into an assignment followed by a *while*-loop. The derivation of the textual inscription is omitted.

The example comprises all the ingredients of the computational framework of *while*-programming (see, e.g., Kfoury, Moll, and Arbib [KMA82]).

8.2   Regulated Rule Application

Usually a set of rules does not suffice to describe the desired computation. In grammatical frameworks, derivations start in some initial configuration and end in terminal configurations. In the area of Petri nets, the firing of transitions begins with an initial marking. In the area of term rewriting, only ground terms or reduced terms are accepted as results of evaluations. Moreover, sometimes one likes to regulate the process of rule application. Examples are the parallel mode of rewriting in L systems and evaluation strategies for terms like *leftmost-innermost* or *parallel-outermost*.

Formally, let C be a set of *control conditions* where a control condition $C \in \mathcal{C}$ provides a binary relation $SEM(C) \subseteq \mathcal{K} \times \mathcal{K}$ as semantics.

This allows to consider a pair (P, C) consisting of a set $P \subseteq \mathcal{R}$ of rules and a control condition $C \in \mathcal{C}$ as a *rule-based system* with the intersection of $\xRightarrow[P]{*}$ and $SEM(C)$ as relational semantics:

$$SEM(P, C) = \xRightarrow[P]{*} \cap \; SEM(C).$$

8.3 Input-output Relations

A typical example of a control condition is a pair (I, T) where I specifies a set $\mathcal{K}(I) \subseteq \mathcal{K}$ of *initial configurations* and T a set $\mathcal{K}(T) \subseteq \mathcal{K}$ of *terminal configurations*. Then the system $(P, (I, T))$ models an input-output relation by

$$SEM(P, (I, T)) = \underset{P}{\overset{*}{\Longrightarrow}} \cap (\mathcal{K}(I) \times (\mathcal{K}(T)).$$

This notion covers many computational models like, e.g., Turing machines, term rewrite systems, graph transformation systems and others.

In this case, the rule application graph can also be extended as an alternative semantics by $Graph(P, (I, T)) = (\mathcal{K}, \underset{P}{\overset{*}{\Longrightarrow}}, \mathcal{K}(I), \mathcal{K}(T))$ where the nodes corresponding to initial and terminal configurations are distinguished accordingly.

Example

In Figure 8.3, the rules from Figure 8.1 are supplemented by an initial flow diagram consisting of a single empty box. Everything except the empty box and the nonterminal letters e and b are accepted as terminal configurations. This rule-based system specifies the language of *while*-programs in form of well-structured flow diagrams as all terminal configurations that are derivable from the only initial diagram by the given rules.

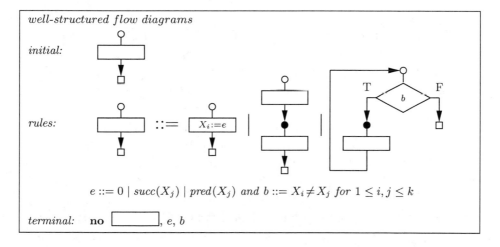

Figure 8.3: A rule-based system specifying all well-structured flow diagrams

8.4   Interpreter Semantics

Rules and control conditions together with the rule application graphs or the iterated rule application relations provide the framework for interpreter semantics. Typically, an abstract interpreter is specified in some rule-based language. If the abstract syntax of a language is represented by textual expressions or terms, the same representation is usually used for the states of the interpreter and term rewrite rules to model the operations of the interpreter. Analogously, if the abstract syntax of a model is represented by diagrams or graphs, it is useful to represent the states of the interpreter by graphs and to model its operations by graph transformation rules (see, e.g., [BMST99, KGKK02, TE00]).

In the latter case, two main approaches are distinguished. Graph transformation rules may be used as the graphical counterparts of classical approaches to semantics like rewriting logic [Mes92] or the chemical abstract machine [BB92], while graphical deduction rules follow the structural operational semantics paradigm. The former are often simpler to write because each rule represents a complete interpreter step (see, e.g., [HHS04, HM00]), while the latter allow a more modular view of the behavior (see, e.g., [CHM00, EHHS00, HZ01]).

Example

The semantics of a *while*-program with the variables $X_1, \ldots, X_k$ can be modeled by state transformation. Since the variables are global and all of the type of natural numbers, a state is a vector $(n_1, \ldots, n_k) \in \mathbb{N}^k$. An arbitrary initial state can be chosen. The evaluation starts at the entry and follows the unique control flow where the current node is indicated by a respective pointer in each case. If the current node is followed by the assignment $X_i := e$, the expression is evaluated according to the actual state and the resulting value is assigned to X_i yielding the new current state. If the current node is followed by a decision with the Boolean expression $X_i \neq X_j$, the actual state is not changed. But the new current node depends on the evaluation of $X_i \neq X_j$ according to the actual state. It is the target of the T-edge if $n_i \neq n_j$ and the target of the F-edge otherwise. The rules in Figure 8.4 describe these evaluation steps. The initial configurations are *well-structured flow diagrams* with a current pointer at the entry together with a simple graphical representation of a state. The evaluation terminates if no further rule is applicable, meaning that the reached configuration is in *reduced form*. This is the case if and only if the current pointer has reached

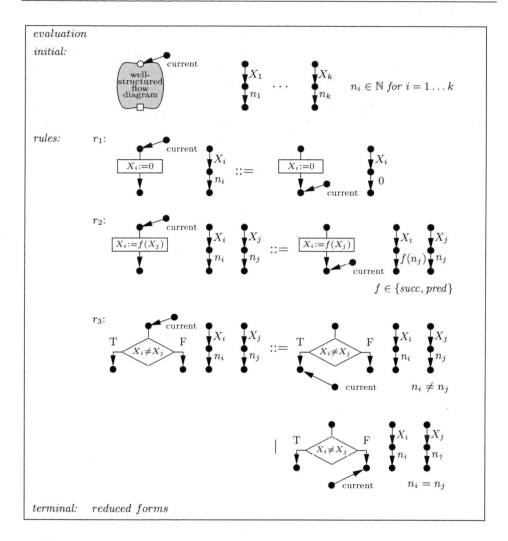

Figure 8.4: Rule-based evaluation of well-structured flow diagrams

the exit. In this way, Figure 8.4 provides an example of an interpreter semantics for visual models.

8.5 Model Transformation

If $\mathcal{K}(I)$ and $\mathcal{K}(T)$ in Section 8.2 are sets of (syntactic representations of) models of some kind, $SEM(P,(I,T))$ is a rule-based model transformation semantics. An example of this type is the translation of sequence diagrams into collaboration diagrams in [CHK04]. Another example is the translation of a complete UML model comprising different diagrams into a set of graph transformation units as presented in [HZG06, ZHG05a, ZHG05b]. This translation yields a semantically equivalent model that can be executed by actually applying the specified rules to a suitable initial system state. A further translation into another graph transformation system with integrated animation information allows for a user-defined animation of the executed model ([EHKZ05]).

Model transformation resembles the situation of denotational semantics if $\mathcal{K}(I)$ is a set of syntactic items while $\mathcal{K}(T)$ is a set of representations of semantic entities. In this case, the rule-based transformation assigns a meaning to each syntactic item according to its structure. Examples of this kind are the translations of sequence and collaboration diagrams into meta model object diagrams in [CHK04] (cf. [BRJ98]).

Various proposals to use graph transformation as a framework for model transformation point in this direction (see, e.g., [AK02, dLV02, Var02] and also [Pra71, Sch95] for earlier approaches).

Example

Besides the visual representation as well-structured flow diagrams, *while*-programs can also be represented textually in the usual style of imperative programs. Figure 8.5 presents a rule-based transformation of the visual models into the textual ones. The initial configurations are well-structured flow diagrams with a translate pointer at the entry. The rules transform the diagram step by step into a string graph that consists of a simple path from the entry to the exit. The edges of this path are labeled with pieces of program texts. The textual *while*-program is obtained by reading the labels along the path. The translation follows the directions of the edges. An assignment statement is easily translated because only the assignment must be kept as edge label and the translate pointer placed to the target. The other two rules deal with the case that the translate pointer faces a decision diamond. In this case, the edges of the *while*-statement as well as the following statement must be translated and put together in the proper order. The translation terminates in reduced forms (i.e. no rule is applicable anymore), which is only the case if the translate pointer has reached the exit.

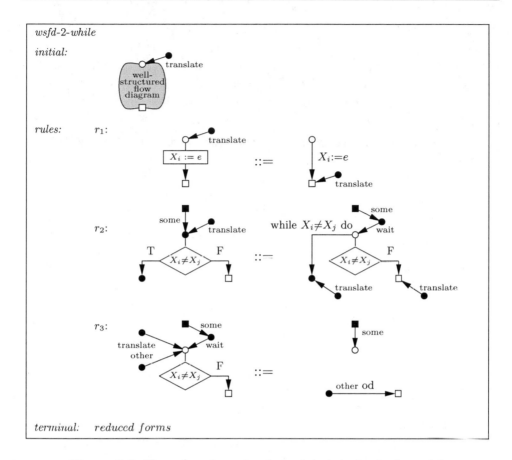

Figure 8.5: Transforming visual models into textual models

8.6 Denotational and Compiler Semantics

The idea of compiler semantics is to translate each program, specification, or model of the source language into an executable program, specification, or model of a target language. The executability of the target language may be described by means of an interpreter semantics. In the case of a visual modeling language, the executable entity can be given by a set of graph transformation rules working on the graph-based representations of the states of the model (see, e.g., [Kre93, Kus01, MSP94]).

Semantics defined as a mapping from the abstract syntax into some semantic domain is referred to as denotational. According to this definition, the compiler semantics is denotational as well, with a semantic domain that is itself operational. If possible, the mapping of programs, specifications, or models into the semantic domain should be defined separately for each element of the abstract syntax so that the meaning of the complete entity can be assembled from the meaning of its elements. This compositionality principle is typical for denotational semantics of programming languages and it is the basis for modular verification, analysis, and evoluation of models (see, e.g., [EHKG02]).

Assuming that the abstract syntax of visual models is represented by graphs, a mapping from graphs to graphs (if the semantic domain happens to have a diagrammatic syntax, like e.g. Petri nets) or from graphs to text (if the semantic domain is algebraic or logic-based, like a process calculus) has to specified. For both variants, different forms of graph transformation rules can be found in the literature (see, e.g., [Bar97, EKHG01, EHK01]).

Example

The model transformation in Figure 8.5 may be seen as a simple example of a compiler that translates visual source programs into textual target programs.

Moreover, *while*-programs have a proper denotational semantics as well. In Figure 8.4, the function on the state space computed by a *while*-program is specified by a rule-based interpreter that evaluates a *while*-program for some input state by traversing the diagram in the proper way. In contrast to this, the denotational semantics reflects the syntactic structure of well-structured flow diagrams as given by the rules in Figure 8.3. If the mapping that assigns the computed function on states to each well-structured flow diagram is denoted by $[\![\ ]\!]$, then $[\![\ ]\!]$ can be defined by some kind of graphical rules as given in Figure 8.6.

8.7 Language Generation and Recognition

A single configuration (with $\mathcal{K}(S) = \{S\}$) provides an interesting special case of a specification of initial configurations. The relational semantics becomes

$$SEM(P, (S, T)) = \{S\} \times \{con \in \mathcal{K}(T) \mid S \xRightarrow[P]{*} con\}.$$

As the first component of each pair of configurations is S, only the second components are significant. In other words, the system $(P, (S, T))$ can be considered as a grammar or language-generation device with

$$L(P, (S, T)) = \{con \in \mathcal{K}(T) \mid S \xRightarrow[P]{*} con\}.$$

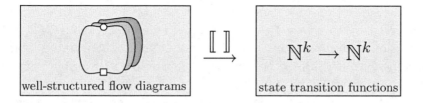

rules :

1.
$$\left[\!\!\left[\begin{array}{c} \circ \\ \boxed{X_i:=0} \\ \downarrow \\ \square \end{array}\right]\!\!\right] (n_1, \ldots, n_k) = (n_1, \ldots, n_{i-1}, 0, n_{i+1}, \ldots, n_k)$$

2.
$$\left[\!\!\left[\begin{array}{c} \circ \\ \boxed{X_i:=f(X_j)} \\ \downarrow \\ \square \end{array}\right]\!\!\right] (n_1, \ldots, n_k) = (n_1, \ldots, n_{i-1}, f(n_j), n_{i+1}, \ldots, n_k)$$

3.
$$\left[\!\!\left[\;\right]\!\!\right] (n_1, \ldots, n_k) = \left[\!\!\left[\;\right]\!\!\right] \left(\left[\!\!\left[\;\right]\!\!\right] (n_1, \ldots, n_k)\right)$$

4.

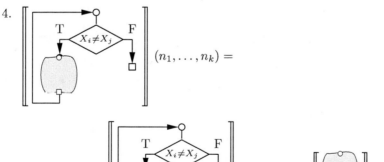

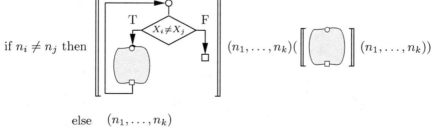

else $\quad (n_1, \ldots, n_k)$

Figure 8.6: Denotational semantics of well-structured flow diagrams

Indeed, most notions of grammars that can be found in the literature are covered by this case of a rule-based system. Elementary net and place/transition systems are further examples of this kind where all cases resp. markings are considered as terminal. A particular example specifying the language of well-structured flow diagrams is given in Figure 8.3. In [EHKG02], the set of all UML sequence diagrams is generated as a language by means of graph transformation rules from an initial graph.

The recognition of languages can be modeled similarly. Finite state automata and pushdown automata are examples of this kind.

8.8   Concluding Remark

In this chapter, some basic aspects of the semantics of rule-based systems and of visual modeling have been discussed. It has been sketched how interpreters and compilers as well as operational and denotational semantics of visual models can be seen as special cases of model transformation and hence defined as rule-based systems. This may be considered as one of the first steps into the systematic investigation of the semantics of visual modeling. Further topics like correctness, modularity, compositionality, and others should be included in the future studies. The structuring concepts of transformation unit (see, e.g.,[KK99b, KKS97]) may be helpful in this respect.

Chapter 9

Excursus: Undecidable Control Conditions

As introduced in Chapter 1 and 3, graph transformation units and autonomous units are approach-independent concepts for structured computation with graph transformation and for rule-based systems in general. On this conceptual level, they are more general than other programming environments for graph transformation, such as, for instance, PROGRES [SWZ99] or AGG [ERT99]. Consequently, a graph transformation unit may be specified over any graph transformation approach, where the approach determines the class of graphs to be worked on, graph transformation rules, and the application of the rules to the graphs.

When trying to calculate the semantics of a transformation unit or the computation of a community of autonomous units, the termination of the derivation process is essential. In [Plu98] it is shown that it is generally undecidable whether a graph transformation derivation terminates. In the meantime, several methods of restricting graph transformation systems in order to tackle the termination problem have been investigated. Concrete termination criteria based on the number of nodes and edges have been presented in [Aßm00]. A general approach based on measurement functions can be found in [BKPT05]. This work is extended and formalized in [EEdL+05]. The termination criteria proposed in the latter two have been implemented as termination checks in the AGG system.

In order to implement the approach-independent concept of graph transformation units and autonomous units so that they may actually be employed for graph transformation programming, the decidability resp. computability of the various components of a unit have to be considered. Obviously, it must be decidable whether a graph is initial or terminal, and whether a rule is applicable to a graph. Moreover, the result of a rule application must be computable. Requiring full decidability for control conditions would, however, be too restrictive since it excludes arbitrary iteration, which is necessary to obtain computational completeness.

In the following three well-known types of control conditions are discussed (as presented in [HKK08]), namely regular expressions over rules and imported transformation units, *as-long-as-possible* on other control conditions, and priorities over rules and imported transformation units, all of which regulate the transformation process. Note, however, that formally any device may be used as a control condition, as long as it specifies a sequence of graphs. An example for this is a sequence of transformation units, specifying the concatenation of the respective semantics and thus a sequence of graphs.

9.1   Modeling Decision Problems

The type graph for the following models is extremely simple. There is only one node type **Node** and one edge type **edge**. The latter is equipped with a string attribute **label**. A *string graph* is a straightforward graph representation of a string $s = a_1 \ldots a_n$. It consists of $n+1$ nodes $v_1, \ldots v_{n+1}$ and n edges $e_1, \ldots, e_n$, where the edge e_i leads from the node v_i to the node v_{i+1} for $i \in \{1, \ldots, n\}$. Every edge e_i is labeled with the symbol a_i. Figure 9.1 shows a sample string graph in compact notion for the string $s = abba$. Identifiers of nodes and edges are omitted, and the nodes are depicted as circles.

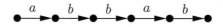

Figure 9.1: A string graph

9.1.1   Modeling Post's Correspondence Problem

An instance of *Post's Correspondence Problem* (PCP), see, e.g., [HMU01], consists of two lists $U = u_1, \ldots, u_k$ and $V = v_1, \ldots, v_k$ of strings over some alphabet Δ, with the two lists being of equal length k. For each i, the pair (u_i, v_i) is a *corresponding* pair. This instance of PCP *has a*

Figure 9.2: Prefix graphs $G(i_1)$ and $G(i_1 i_2)$

solution if there is a nonempty sequence $i_1 \cdots i_n \in \{1, \ldots, k\}$ such that $u_{i_1} \cdots u_{i_n} = v_{i_1} \cdots v_{i_n}$.

The search for a solution of such a given instance of PCP is modeled by successively adding corresponding pairs to a prefix graph. Such a prefix graph consists of two disjoint string graphs. Moreover, the prefix graph contains a B-labeled edge from the first node of the first string graph to the first node of the second string graph, and an E-labeled edge analogously connecting the respective last nodes of the string graphs. If we have for instance $u_{i_1} = ba$, $u_{i_2} = a$, $v_{i_1} = b$, $v_{i_2} = aab$, the graphs in Figure 9.2 are prefix graphs $\mathcal{G}(i_1)$ and $\mathcal{G}(i_1 i_2)$, respectively. The rule for the corresponding pair i_2 is depicted in Figure 9.3.

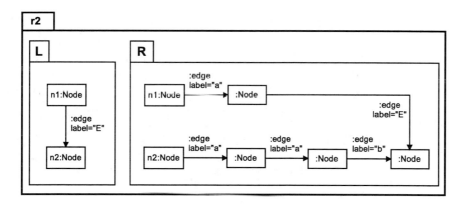

Figure 9.3: Rule r_2

In general, each corresponding pair (u_i, v_i) gives rise to a rule r_i as sketched in Figure 9.4. Here, an "edge" with a whole string w on it refers to the respective string graph. Starting with the prefix graph $G()$ for the empty prefix, which consists of two nodes and two parallel edges between them with labels B and E, respectively, the derivation

$$G() \overset{*}{\Longrightarrow} G(i_1 \cdots i_m) \underset{r_{i_{m+1}}}{\Longrightarrow} G(i_1 \cdots i_{m+1})$$

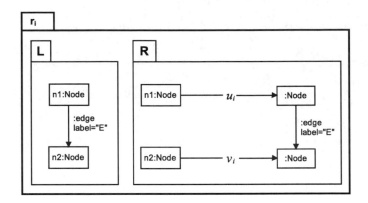

Figure 9.4: Rule r_i

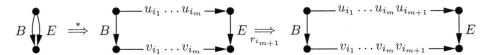

Figure 9.5: Deriving prefix graphs for a PCP instance

is sketched in Figure 9.5.

Of course, this process can produce any index sequence. So it must be combined with verifying the correctness of a solution. This will be done using deconstructing rules r_x, one for each $x \in \Delta$, as shown in Figure 9.6.

Now these rules have to be combined in a useful way. This will be done in a so-called *graph transformation unit*, as shown in Figure 9.7.

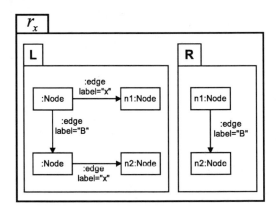

Figure 9.6: The PCP rule r_x for $x \in \Delta$

PCP
initial $G()$
rules r_i for $i = 1, \ldots, k$
r_{x_j} for $\Delta = \{x_1, \ldots, x_l\}$ and $j = 1, \ldots, l$
conds $(r_1 \mid \ldots \mid r_k \mid r_{x_1} \mid \ldots \mid r_{x_l})^+$
terminal $G()$

Figure 9.7: The graph transformation unit for a PCP instance

Informally, the meaning of this unit may be described as follows: Any derivation starts in an *initial* graph, here always $G()$. The given *rules* may then be applied according to the *control condition*, which is here a regular expression over the rules that allows any sequence of rules except the empty sequence, i.e. at least one rule application must be executed. Since there is no couple of edges in $G()$ that can be deleted by any of the rules r_x for $x \in \Delta$, the first rule must be one of the constructive rules r_i. The derivation may stop whenever a *terminal* graph, here again always $G()$, is reached. Thus, in between a double string is constructed from the corresponding pairs by applying the rules r_i, and deconstructed as long as the symbols correspond by applying the rules r_x. The semantics of the unit then contains all pairs of initial and terminal graphs such that there is a derivation from the initial to the terminal graph that obeys the control condition. In this concrete case, the semantics of **PCP** contains only the pair of the unique initial and unique terminal graph, i.e. $(G(), G())$, if and only if the PCP instance has a solution. Otherwise the semantics is empty.

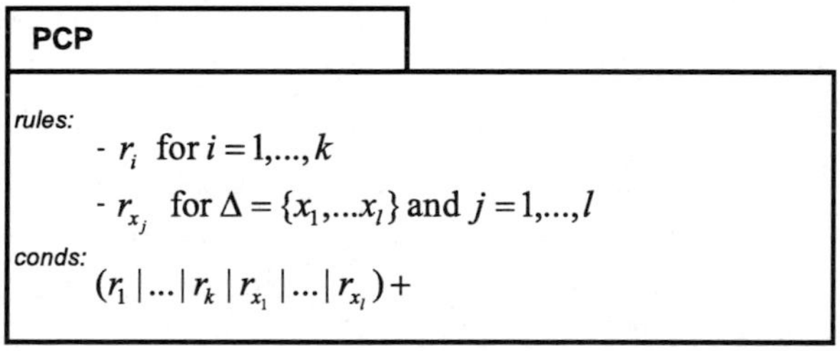

PCP

rules:
- r_i for $i = 1, \ldots, k$
- r_{x_j} for $\Delta = \{x_1, \ldots x_l\}$ and $j = 1, \ldots, l$

conds:
$(r_1 \mid \ldots \mid r_k \mid r_{x_1} \mid \ldots \mid r_{x_l})+$

Figure 9.8: The PCP unit

The PCP model may also be realized as a community *COM* of autonomous units. The autonomous unit PCP, as depicted in Figure 9.8, is the sole member of this community. It has no explicit goal, and the same rules and control condition as the transformation unit specified above. The community then has the goal $G()$ which is also the initial environment. The semantics of the transformation unit above is then the same as the community semantics $REL_{Seq}(COM)$.

9.1.2 Modeling Turing Machines

Turing machines are formal models that are frequently used to show results in computation and complexity theory. They have also been used to prove properties of graph transformation systems. For instance in [HP01] a Turing machine is simulated by a graph transformation program to show the computational completeness of a newly developed graph transformation-based programming language.

A Turing machine M is a device that is in one of various states at any given instant. It contains a linear tape, comprising a chain of cells which are ordered from left to right. A cell can be empty or it can contain a symbol from a given finite alphabet Σ. The alphabet Σ' contains all symbols from Σ and the special symbol $\sqcup$ (denoting an empty cell). At any time the tape is finitely long, but it may be extended to the left and right with empty cells under certain circumstances. The Turing machine also includes a read-write head which is positioned on one of the cells. For this reason the tape can be described by two strings $u, v \in \Sigma'^*$. The string u contains the tape content that is left of the current head position, and v the tape content to its right including the current cell. Initially the machine is in a distinguished start state q_0, the head is positioned at the leftmost cell and no cell is empty if $v \neq \lambda$ (i.e. $u = \lambda$ and $v \in \Sigma^*$). The action of the Turing machine is determined by a configuration transition relation δ that assigns a new state q', a symbol σ', and a direction $d \in \{L, R\}$ to a current state q and a symbol σ. A concrete step of a Turing machine then changes the state, writes a symbol into the current cell and moves the head to the left or to the right, always according to the configuration transition relation. Such a step can be repeatedly executed until no further step is possible. This is obviously the case if δ does not specify a transition for the given state and the scanned symbol. This happens in particular if the current state of the machine is a final state. In case the head is positioned on the leftmost cell and δ specifies a movement of the head to the left, the tape is extended to the left by one empty cell and the head positioned on this new cell. This is done analogously for the right end of the tape. An advanced introduction to Turing machines, different existing types, and their properties can be found in, e.g., [HMU01].

Formally, a *Turing machine* is a tuple $M = (Q, \Sigma, \Sigma', \delta, q_0, F)$. Here Q is a finite set of states, Σ is a finite alphabet, $\Sigma' = \Sigma \cup \{\sqcup\}$, δ is a configuration transition relation, $q_0 \in Q$ is the start state, and $F \subseteq Q$ is a set of final states (we will assume w.l.o.g. that $F = \{q_\mathrm{F}\}$). The configuration transition relation δ assigns a new state q', a symbol $\sigma' \in \Sigma'$, and a direction $d \in \{L, R\}$ to a current state q and a symbol $\sigma \in \Sigma'$. It is thus $\delta : Q \times \Sigma' \rightsquigarrow Q \times \Sigma' \times \{L, R\}$ with $(q, \sigma) \mapsto (q', \sigma', d)$.

The current state of the Turing machine, the position of the head on the tape and the contents of the tape form the current *configuration* of the Turing machine, which can be denoted by a single string. Let $uv \in \Sigma'^*$ denote the tape content as explained above, with the head currently on the first symbol of v (or an empty cell if $v = \lambda$). Then the current state q_i of the machine is inserted into this string yielding $uq_i v$ as a string representation of the configuration. For this notation we obviously assume that the identifiers of the states are different from the symbols of the alphabet. An initial configuration of a Turing machine M is of the form $\lambda q_0 w$ with $w \in \Sigma^*$. A final configuration is of the form $uq_\mathrm{F} v$ with $u, v \in \Sigma'^*$ and $q_\mathrm{F} \in F$. For states in F the configuration transition relation must not specify a next state. Let $q, q' \in Q$, $u, v \in \Sigma'^*$, and $a, b, c \in \Sigma'$. A next configuration then emerges as follows:

- $uqav \mapsto ubq'v$ for $(q, a, q', b, R) \in \delta$

- $uq\lambda \mapsto uq\sqcup$

- $ucqav \mapsto uq'cbv$ for $(q, a, q', b, L) \in \delta$

- $\lambda qav \mapsto q' \sqcup bv$ for $(q, a, q', b, L) \in \delta$

Here a transformation unit which models an arbitrary Turing machine is considered. For the graph representation of the tape a string graph is used. For technical reasons it is also necessary to be able to determine whether the head is positioned on the leftmost resp. rightmost cell. For this reason we introduce two special cells labeled $\triangleright$ (indicating the left end) and $\triangleleft$ (indicating the right end). The head can never be placed on these special cells.

The current configuration of the Turing machine can then be represented as a graph in the following way. Let q_i be the current state of the machine, $w = \alpha_1 \alpha_2 \ldots \alpha_n$ be the content of the tape, and the head be positioned on the cell containing α_1. Then the string graph representing the content of the tape is extended by adding an edge parallel to the edge labeled α_1. This new edge is then labeled with the state q_i. Figure 9.9 shows the graph representing the initial state of the Turing machine $q_0 w$ with $w = \alpha_1 \alpha_2 \ldots \alpha_n$.

Figure 9.9: The graph representing $q_0 w$

The initial configuration $q_0 \lambda$ with the empty word λ as tape content is represented as depicted in Figure 9.10.

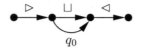

Figure 9.10: Graph representation of $q_0 \lambda$

For the dynamics of the Turing machine one graph transformation rule for every transition of the modeled Turing machine is defined. In order to obtain a generic framework for the modeling of a Turing machine, we combine analogous rules. Let $M = (Q, \Sigma, \Sigma', \delta, q_0, F)$ be the Turing machine to be modeled. Then for every transition $(q, \sigma, q', \sigma', R) \in \delta$ two different rules are needed as depicted in Figure 9.11. The first rule specifies the ordinary replacement of σ with σ', the movement of the head to the right and the change of the state q to q'. Here τ is left unchanged by the rule, since it is a variable label that matches every symbol from Σ'. The second rule is needed in case the head is positioned on the right end of the tape. In this case a new empty cell is inserted and the head placed upon it. Combine the first kind of rules to form rule set R_1, and the second kind of rules to form rule set R_2.

These rules are already sufficient to model every step of the configuration transition relation which specifies a movement of the head to the right. In order to model those steps that contain a head movement to the left, two sets R_3 and R_4 of different rules also have to be created. Create two rules for all $(q, \sigma, q', \sigma', L)$ as depicted in Figure 9.12. Again two rules are needed for every combination, because it may be necessary to extend the tape to its left.

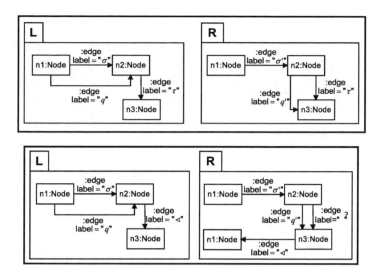

Figure 9.11: Two rules for every $(q, \sigma, q', \sigma', R)$

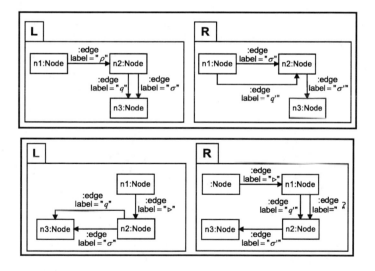

Figure 9.12: Two rules for every $(q, \sigma, q', \sigma', L)$

The final rule that is needed for this example is a rule which resets a final state of the Turing machine to the initial state, neither changing the contents of the tape nor the position of the head. This is realized by the rule r_f depicted in Figure 9.13.

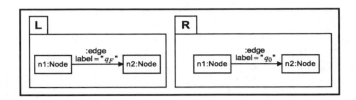

Figure 9.13: Rule to reset a final state to the initial state

The transformation unit that realizes a Turing machine is depicted in Figure 9.14. As initial graphs we consider all string graphs for configurations with the initial state q_0, including in particular all encodings of initial configurations. The union of the rule sets R_1, R_2, R_3 and R_4 forms the set R. So the transformation unit contains all of them as rules, plus the final-state-resetting rule r_f. The control condition allows to select any one of the rules from the rule set $R = \{r_1, \ldots, r_k\}$ and repeat this selection arbitrarily often. After that repetition the rule r_f has to be applied. It is noteworthy that this rule can only be applied if the Turing machine simulation has actually reached the final state q_F. Thus, the semantics of this unit contains, among others, all pairs (G, H) such that G represents an initial configuration $q_0 w$ and H represents some accepting configuration that M can reach on input w, but with the initial instead of the final state.

tu(M)
initial $\{\triangleright w_1 q_0 w_2 \triangleleft \mid w_1, w_2 \in \Sigma'^*\}$
rules $R \cup \{r_f\}$
conds $(r_1 \mid \ldots \mid r_k)^*; r_f$

Figure 9.14: The graph transformation unit for a Turing machine M

The model of the Turing machine may also be realized as a community *COM* of autonomous units. The autonomous unit TU is the sole member of this community. It has no explicit goal, and the same rules and control condition as the transformation unit specified above. The community then has the same initial environment as the transformation unit **tu(m)**. The overall goal is an environment, in which one edge with the label q_0 exists. The semantics of the transformation unit **tu(m)** is then the same as the community semantics $REL_{Seq}(COM)$.

9.2 Decidability of Control Conditions

Control conditions regulate the control flow along rule applications and use of imported transformation units. Various kinds of control conditions and the interrelations between them are studied in [Kus00a]. Three kinds of control conditions have proved to be particularly useful in numerous examples: regular expressions, *as-long-as-possible*, and priorities. In this section, we will study these kinds of control conditions under the aspect of decidability.

Let $\mathcal{G}$ be a class of graphs, E an identifier semantics and $C \in \mathcal{C}$ a control condition with $SEM_E(C) \subseteq Seq(\mathcal{G})$. Then C is *decidable* if there is an algorithm that decides, for any $(G, H) \in \mathcal{G} \times \mathcal{G}$, whether a sequence $s = (G_i)_{i \in [n]} \in SEM_E(C)$ exists with $G = G_0$ and $H = G_n$. C is called *(positive) semi-decidable* if there is a procedure that on input $(G, H) \in \mathcal{G} \times \mathcal{G}$ will eventually halt if a sequence $s = (G_i)_{i \in [n]} \in SEM_E(C)$ exists with $G = G_0$ and $H = G_n$, and give the correct answer to the question '$(G_i)_{i \in [n]} \in SEM_E(C)$ with $G = G_0$ and $H = G_n$?' whenever it halts.

9.2.1 Regular Expressions

Consider the set ID which contains only the identifiers ID_R of the given rules and the identifiers ID_U of imported transformation units. Each regular expression over ID denotes a regular language of strings over ID, and intuitively each of these strings describes a possible sequence of rule applications interleaved with calls of imported units.

The set REX of regular expressions over ID is defined as usual: $\emptyset$ and λ are regular expressions, each $id \in ID$ is a regular expression, and $(e_1; e_2)$, $(e_1 | e_2)$, (e^*) are regular expressions for all expressions $e_1, e_2, e \in REX$. A regular expression is *star-free* if it does not contain a subexpression of the form (e^*).

In order to avoid parentheses, we assume that '$*$' has a stronger binding than '$;$', which in turn has a stronger binding than '$|$'. Moreover, '$;$' and '$|$' are associative, so that corresponding parentheses may be dropped too.

In the context of this chapter the intermediate steps in the graph sequence allowed by a control condition are of no interest. For this reason, the semantics of a control condition is here defined as a binary relation on graphs. This is no contradiction to the previous definitions, but a different point of view. Instead of taking the whole sequence as semantics, in this context only the first and last graph of the sequence are considered.

Formally, the semantics of a regular expression as control condition in the context of this chapter is a binary relation on $\mathcal{G}$ that is inductively defined as follows: For $\emptyset$, λ, and $id \in ID$, we have

- $SEM(\emptyset) = \emptyset$,

- $SEM(\lambda) = \{(G, G) \mid G \in \mathcal{G}\}$

- $SEM(id) = E(id)$, i.e. the relation assigned by the identifier semantics.

Then for $e, e_1, e_2 \in REX$ we have

- $SEM(e_1; e_2) = \{(G, H) \mid \exists\, G' \in CG : (G, G') \in SEM(e_1) \text{ and } (G', H) \in SEM(e_2)\}$,

- $SEM(e_1 | e_2) = \{(G, H) \mid (G, H) \in SEM(e_1) \text{ or } (G, H) \in SEM(e_2)\}$, and

- $SEM(e^*) = \{(G, H) \mid \exists\, n \geq 1, G_0, \ldots, G_n \in \mathcal{G} \text{ with } (G_{i-1}, G_i) \in SEM(e) \text{ for } i = 1, \ldots, n \text{ such that } G_0 = G \text{ and } G_n = H\} \cup \{(G, G) \mid G \in \mathcal{G}\}$.

For instance, the control condition of the transformation unit **PCP** in Figure 9.7 is a regular expression, where the convention is used that for a given regular expression e the expression e^+ abbreviates $e; e^*$.

Decidability of regular expressions.

The following observations can be made:

1. If C is a star-free regular expression over ID_R, it describes a finite language over rules. Due to the assumption in Section 3 that rule applicability must be decidable, rule application computable, and that all objects are finite, this implies that such a control condition is decidable.

2. If C is a regular expression over ID_R containing a star, it defines an infinite (but enumerable) language over rules and is therefore (with the same argument as above) semi-decidable. However, in general it is not decidable: As a counterexample, consider the control condition $C_{\mathbf{PCP}}$ of **PCP**, which is of this kind and does not allow to decide whether $(G(); G())$ is in the semantics of $C_{\mathbf{PCP}}$ since PCP is undecidable.

3. Any identifier for a transformation unit with decidable finite semantics may additionally occur in a regular expression and the statements above still hold.

4. Any identifier for a transformation unit with decidable, but infinite semantics in an otherwise (semi-)decidable control condition will lead to a semi-decidable semantics.

5. Any identifier for a transformation unit with undecidable semantics turns a regular expression into an undecidable control condition.

9.2.2 As-long-as-possible

Given any control condition C, the idea of *as-long-as-possible* is to iterate that condition until it can no longer be totally executed. For instance, if $C = r_1; r_2$ is a sequence of two rules, the iteration $(r_1; r_2)!$ stops when this sequence cannot be applied anymore, even if r_1 alone could still be applied.

Let C be some control condition. Then $C!$ defines the set of all pairs $(G, H) \in SEM_E(C)^*$ such that no $H' \in \mathcal{G}$ exists with $(H, H') \in SEM_E(C)$.

For instance, one might replace the control condition of **tu(M)** in Figure 9.14 with $(r_1 | \ldots | r_k)!$. Then the semantics of that unit changes to include, among others, all pairs of graphs (G, H) where G represents an initial configuration on which the Turing machine will eventually halt, and H is such a halting configuration (whether accepting or not).

Decidability of as-long-as-possible.

The following observations can be made:

1. Iterating a star-free regular expression over rules with *as-long-as-possible* yields a semi-decidable control condition. It is in general not decidable because the halting problem for Turing machines is only semi-decidable, and that is what the variant of the Turing machine simulation given above encodes. It is still semi-decidable since star-free regular expressions over rules are decidable.

2. Iterating a single imported transformation unit using a control condition with *as-long-as-possible* is in general undecidable and not even semi-decidable. Consider the control condition **PCP!**, where **PCP** is the unit in Figure 9.7, and the question whether $(G(), G()) \in SEM_E(\mathbf{PCP!})$. If the encoded PCP has a solution, then $SEM(\mathbf{PCP}) = \{(G(), G())\}$, and $(G(), G()) \notin SEM_E(\mathbf{PCP!})$. If the PCP does

not have a solution, then $SEM(\mathbf{PCP}) = \emptyset$ and therefore $(G(), G()) \in SEM_E(\mathbf{PCP!})$. But this is not semi-decidable.

It may seem that the undecidability of *as-long-as-possible* iterating only a single transformation unit is due to the nondeterminism used in the control condition of **PCP** for the choice of the next constructive rule (the next applicable deconstructing rule is always dependent on the symbol appearing next to the B-labeled edge). However, this is not the case, which may be seen by considering $\mathbf{tu(M)}$: Since decidability questions are of greater interest than complexity, it may be assumed w.l.o.g. that M is a deterministic Turing machine. Consequently, any derivation in $\mathbf{tu(M)}$ is deterministic, too. Yet, the control condition $\mathbf{tu(M)}$! is undecidable by analogous reasoning to the one used above for **PCP**.

9.2.3   Priorities

A priority control condition is a partial order on rules and used units that allows the application of a rule or a unit only if there is no rule or unit of higher priority that can be applied to the current graph.

A priority is a pair $C = (ID, <)$ where $<$ is an irreflexive partial order on ID. For $id \in ID$, let $HP_C(id) = \{id' \in ID \mid id < id'\}$ denote the set of identifiers with higher priority in C. Then $(G, H) \in SEM_E(C)$ if there are $G_0, \ldots, G_n \in \mathcal{G}$ such that

- $G_0 = G$ and $G_n = H$,

- for $i = 1, \ldots, n$, $(G_{i-1}, G_i) \in E(id_i)$ for some $id_i \in ID$, and for all $id \in HP_C(id_i)$ there is no $G \in \mathcal{G}$ with $(G_{i-1}, G) \in E(id)$.

For instance, the control condition of **PCP** might be replaced with one that gives a higher priority to the constructing rules r_i than to the deconstructing rules r_x. Since a constructive rule can always be applied to any graph derived from $G()$, all graphs $G(w)$ where w is a sequence over the indices $1, \ldots, k$ can be derived, without any deconstruction from the side of the B-labeled edge. From such a graph, $G()$ can never be derived again. Nevertheless, the empty derivation ensures that $(G(), G())$ is always in the semantics of the changed unit (and it is the only pair).

Decidability of priorities.

We can make the following observations:

1. Any priority control condition that gives higher priority exclusively to rules is decidable, since the applicability of rules is required to be decidable.

2. Priority control conditions where a higher priority is given to some imported transformation unit are in general not decidable. Consider a rule r that replaces $G()$ with some graph H distinct from $G()$. We want to know whether $(G(), H)$ is in the semantics of the control condition $r < \textbf{PCP}$. If $SEM(\textbf{PCP})$ is empty, we may apply r, and the answer is yes. If $SEM(\textbf{PCP})$ is not empty, it contains (only) the pair $(G(), G())$, and because of the higher priority of $\textbf{PCP}$ we may never apply r, implying that the answer is no. Since the semantics of $\textbf{PCP}$ is undecidable, so is the semantics of the priority control condition $r < \textbf{PCP}$.

9.2.4 Consequences for Implementation

The results of this section rely on the use of a graph transformation approach that is computationally complete. Thus, it is to be expected that decidability of a control condition is the exception rather than the rule.

The semi-decidability of regular expressions over rules is due to the lack of general termination criteria. Consequently, just as with the control flow in ordinary programming languages, it is the responsibility of the programmer to ensure that their control condition in a graph transformation unit will always terminate. This task could be supported by providing tools to verify (the termination of) graph transformation units.

At the heart of the undecidability concerning *as-long-as-possible* or priorities on imported units lies the use of an undecidable condition, which is embodied in the semi- or undecidability of the semantics of the imported unit. At least for a first implementation of graph transformation units and while there is no support yet to prove the decidability for the imported unit, it seems therefore reasonable to syntactically forbid control conditions of this kind.

9.3 Concluding Remark

In this chapter it has been illustrated that certain control conditions used in transformation units and autonomous units are not decidable in general. It turns out that star-free regular expressions over rules are decidable, while regular expressions including the star are in general not decidable, as the

PCP example shows. Iterating a star-free regular expression over rules as well as iterating a single imported transformation unit with *as-long-as-possible* is generally undecidable and the latter is not even semi-decidable. The Turing machine example demonstrates that the undecidability of iterating a single imported transformation unit is not due to nondeterminism in control conditions. Similarly, priority control conditions that assign a higher priority to some imported unit are undecidable, whereas they are decidable if some higher priority is assigned only to rules. Therefore, a first implementation of graph transformation units and autonomous units should disallow *as-long-as-possible* and higher priorities on imported units.

The results presented here are based on the use of a graph transformation approach that is computationally complete. It would be interesting to study the decidability of control conditions for less expressive approaches, in the hope of obtaining more decidability results.

Conclusion

Summary

In this thesis, communities of autonomous units are introduced as a formal modeling concept. The autonomous units that participate in a community represent system components which interact in a rule-based, self-controlled, and goal-driven manner within a common environment. This thesis focuses on the investigation of communities of autonomous units using graph transformation as underlying formal framework. In general, any rule-based mechanism may be used that provides a set of configurations and a set of rules specifying a binary relation on such configurations. Employing such a formal framework, a formal sequential process semantics as well as a formal parallel process semantics for communities of autonomous units are defined. Moreover, some preliminary ideas for the definition of a formal concurrent process semantics are presented.

The notion of communities of autonomous units is first illustrated with two simple examples. In the first example the formal concept of Petri nets is modeled as a community of autonomous units. Here every transition of the Petri net is modeled as one autonomous unit. In the second example a very simple version of a foraging ant colony is modeled. Here every ant of the colony is modeled as an autonomous unit.

Communities of autonomous units are then applied to the domain of transport logistics. As a first application, a transport network is modeled which consists of depots and their connections, unit loads, and trucks. The load units have to be transported from a source depot to a target depot by trucks. In this application, the trucks as well as the load units are modeled as autonomous units. Both kinds of units plan their tours autonomously and a very preliminary negotiation between load units and trucks results in the actual transportation of a load unit by a truck.

The simple negotiation is then extended to a more sophisticated approach based on communication. It is shown that autonomous units can communicate by inserting and replacing corresponding edges in their common environment.

Two case studies that have actually been implemented using the graph transformation engine of the tool **GrGen** are then presented in detail. The first case study deals with a model of the board game Ludo and the sequential process semantics of the corresponding community. Here every player as well as the die is modeled as an autonomous unit. It is shown how different strategies for the players can be specified. Simulation runs show that the use of different player strategies actually influence the result of the game and provide a first insight into advantages and disadvantages of a particular strategy.

The second case study deals with a model of a foraging ant colony and the parallel process semantics of the corresponding community. Here every ant is modeled as an autonomous unit. In this model, ants carrying food deposit pheromones on their memorized way back to the nest. These pheromones then influence foraging ants in the selection of their next path in a probabilistic way. Since the pheromone evaporates over time, this model also comprises a special autonomous unit that models the environment changes that are not induced by the ants. Simulation results show that even a relatively small colony of ants is able to find a shortest path using a suitable setup of the overall system.

Some fundamental aspects of the semantics of rule-based systems in relation to the semantics of visual models are then discussed which form the conceptional background of this thesis.

As the specifications in this thesis show, control conditions are a very important part of the models. For this reason the main challenge of an implementation of autonomous units is the efficient handling of control conditions. It turns out that even seemingly simple control conditions may be harmful, since they can already be undecidable.

Outlook

There are at least the following interesting points for future work.

- The basic idea of autonomous units is that each of them decides for itself which rule is to be applied next. They are independent of each other and the parts of the environment graphs where their rules apply may be far away from each other. Hence a sequential behavior of the community (like in many card and board games) will rarely be adequate. But the parallel behavior does not always reflect the actual situations to be modeled because a parallel step has an explicit begin and end, whereas there may be activities of units that cannot be related to each other with respect to time. A proper concurrent semantics of autonomous units may fix this problem.

- Besides Petri nets, the theory of concurrency offers a wide spectrum of notions of processes like communicating sequential processes, calculus of communicating systems, traces, and bigraphs. A detailed comparison of these concepts with autonomous units can lead to interesting insights.

- Communities of autonomous units should be implemented in order to be able to elaborate and to verify case-studies of realistic size. It has turned out that the tool GrGen is suitable even for large graphs, so it would make sense to use it as the basis for an implementation of autonomous unit on this tool.

- Up to now, the goal of an autonomous unit is defined as a graph class expression. Since for some applications this may not be sufficient, other adequate classes of goals should be studied. It should also be studied which concrete classes of control conditions are suitable or sufficient for autonomous units.

- A remarkable aspect of the classical transformation units is the structuring principle. This is achieved by the import feature of transformation units, which allows them to import other transformation units and utilize them to solve subtasks. So far only autonomous units with sequential semantics have been defined with an additional structuring principle. But it would generally make sense for autonomous units to modularize the solution of a task or to let subtasks be handled by other autonomous units. For this reason, future work should also concentrate on structured autonomous units in the parallel and concurrent cases.

- Since the approach of autonomous units provides a formal modeling concept, it should be investigated whether and how automated verification of system or process properties including termination proofs can be achieved.

- More case studies should be specified. In this context it would be meaningful to investigate one application with several case studies employing different degrees of control distribution.

- Communities of autonomous units that can perform parallel and concurrent transformations should be further investigated. Here results from the theory of graph transformation [EKMR99] may be helpful.

- In order to make autonomous units applicable in practice, it should be investigated whether and how the rules and the control conditions can be correctly translated to existing and practically relevant systems, like e.g. multi-agent systems.

A vision for a future in which autonomous units are applied to practice comprises the following. First the system to be realized is specified as a community of autonomous units. If the common environment of the system can be represented as a graph in a natural way, the use of graph transformation as the underlying rule-based system will allow for a straightforward and intuitive modeling process. Crucial properties of the model are then verified in an automated way and the model can be tested in a suitable simulation environment. Finally, a formally correct translation of the specification into e.g. a system of multi-agents realizes the specification.

Bibliography

[AK02]   D. H. Akehurst and S. Kent. A Relational Approach to Defining
           Transformations in a Metamodel. In Jézéquel et al. [JHC02],
           pages 243–258.

[Aßm00]   U. Aßmann. Graph Rewrite Systems for Program Optimiza-
           tion. *ACM Transactions on programming Languages and Sys-
           tems (TOPLAS)*, 22(4), 2000.

[Bar97]   L. Baresi. *Formal Customization of Graphical Notations*. PhD
           thesis, Dipartimento di Elettronica e Informazione – Politecnico
           di Milano, 1997. In Italian.

[BB92]   G. Berry and G. Boudol. The Chemical Abstract Machine.
           Theoretical Computer Science, 96(1):217–248, 1992.

[BDG92]   R. Beckers, J.-L. Deneubourg, and S. Goss. Trails and U-turns
           in the Selection of a Path by the Ant Lasius Niger. *Journal of
           Theoretical Biology*, 159:397–415, 1992.

[BDT99]   E. Bonabeau, M. Dorigo, and G. Theraulaz. *Swarm Intelli-
           gence, From Natural to Artificial Systems*. Oxford University
           Press, New York, USA, 1999.

[BKPT05]   P. Bottoni, M. Koch, F. Parisi-Presicce, and G. Taentzer. Ter-
           mination of High-Level Replacement Units with Application to
           Model Transformation. *Electronic Notes in Theoretical Com-
           puter Science*, 127(4):71–86, 2005.

[BMST99]   R. Bardohl, M. Minas, Andy Schürr, and G. Taentzer. Appli-
           cation of graph transformation to visual languages. In Ehrig
           et al. [EEKR99], pages 105–180.

[BN98]   F. Baader and T. Nipkow. *Term Rewriting and All That*. Cambridge University Press, Cambridge, UK, 1998.

[BRJ98]   G. Booch, J. Rumbaugh, and I. Jacobson. *The Unified Modeling Language User Guide*. Addison-Wesley, Reading, Massachusetts, USA, 1998.

[CEKR02]   A. Corradini, H. Ehrig, H.-J. Kreowski, and G. Rozenberg, editors. *Graph Transformation, Proceedings of the 1st Intl. Conference on Graph Transformations (ICGT 2002)*, volume 2505 of *Lecture Notes in Computer Science*, Berlin, Heidelberg, 2002. Springer.

[CEM⁺06]   A. Corradini, H. Ehrig, U. Montanari, L. Ribeiro, and G. Rozenberg, editors. *Graph Transformations, Proceedings of the 3rd Intl. Conference on Graph Transformations (ICGT 2006)*, volume 4178 of *Lecture Notes in Computer Science*, Berlin, Heidelberg, 2006. Springer.

[CHK04]   B. Cordes, K. Hölscher, and H.-J. Kreowski. UML Interaction Diagrams: Correct Translation of Sequence Diagrams into Collaboration Diagrams. In J. L. Pfaltz, M. Nagl, and B. Böhlen, editors, *Applications of Graph Transformations with Industrial Relevance, Second International Workshop, AGTIVE 2003, Charlottesville, VA, USA, September 27 - October 1, 2003, Revised Selected and Invited Papers*, volume 3062 of *Lecture Notes in Computer Science*, pages 275–291, Berlin, Heidelberg, 2004. Springer.

[CHM00]   A. Corradini, R. Heckel, and U. Montanari. Graphical Operational Semantics. In Rolim et al. [RBC⁺00], pages 411–418.

[Coo81]   R.B. Cooper. *Introduction to Queueing Theory, 2nd Edition*. Elsevier, New York, USA, 1981.

[DAGP90]   J.-L. Deneubourg, S. Aron, S. Goss, and J.-M. Pasteels. The Self-Organizing Exploratory Pattern of the Argentine Ant. *Journal of Insect Behavior*, 3:159–168, 1990.

[dLV02]   J. de Lara and H. Vangheluwe. AToM³: A Tool for Multi-formalism and Meta-modelling. In R.-D. Kutsche and H. Weber, editors, *Fundamental Approaches to Software Engineering,*

5th International Conference, FASE 2002, held as Part of the
Joint European Conferences on Theory and Practice of Software, ETAPS 2002, Grenoble, France, April 8-12, 2002, Proceedings, volume 2306 of Lecture Notes in Computer Science,
pages 174–188, Berlin, Heidelberg, 2002. Springer.

[DMC91]   M. Dorigo, V. Maniezzo, and A. Colorni. Positive Feedback
          as a Search Strategy. Technical Report 91-016, Politecnico di
          Milano, 1991.

[DMC96]   M. Dorigo, V. Maniezzo, and A. Colorni. The Ant System: Op-
          timization by a Colony of Cooperating Agents. IEEE Transac-
          tions on Systems, Man, and Cybernetics Part B: Cybernetics,
          26(1):29–41, 1996.

[EEdL+05] H. Ehrig, K. Ehrig, J. de Lara, G. Taentzer, D. Varró, and
          S. Varró-Gyapay. Termination Criteria for Model Transforma-
          tion. In M. Cerioli, editor, Fundamental Approaches to Soft-
          ware Engineering, 8th International Conference, FASE 2005,
          Held as Part of the Joint European Conferences on Theory and
          Practice of Software, ETAPS 2005, Edinburgh, UK, April 4-8,
          2005, Proceedings, volume 3442 of Lecture Notes in Computer
          Science, pages 49–63, Berlin, Heidelberg, 2005. Springer.

[EEKR99] H. Ehrig, G. Engels, H.-J. Kreowski, and G. Rozenberg, edi-
          tors. Handbook of Graph Grammars and Computing by Graph
          Transformation, Vol. 2: Applications, Languages and Tools,
          volume 2. World Scientific, Singapore, 1999.

[EEPT06] H. Ehrig, K. Ehrig, U. Prange, and G. Taentzer. Fundamen-
          tals of Algebraic Graph Transformation. EATCS Monographs
          in Theoretical Computer Science. Springer, Berlin, Heidelberg,
          2006.

[EHHS00] G. Engels, J. Hendrik Hausmann, R. Heckel, and S. Sauer. Dy-
          namic Meta Modeling: A Graphical Approach to the Opera-
          tional Semantics of Behavioral Diagrams in UML. In A. Evans,
          S. Kent, and B. Selic, editors, UML 2000 - The Unified Mod-
          eling Language, Advancing the Standard, Third International
          Conference, York, UK, October 2-6, 2000, Proceedings, vol-
          ume 1939 of Lecture Notes in Computer Science, pages 323–
          337, Berlin, Heidelberg, 2000. Springer.

[EHK+97]   H. Ehrig, R. Heckel, M. Korff, M. Löwe, L. Ribeiro, A. Wagner, and A. Corradini. Algebraic Approaches to Graph Transformation - Part II: Single Pushout Approach and Comparison with Double Pushout Approach. In Rozenberg [Roz97], pages 247–312.

[EHK01]   G. Engels, R. Heckel, and J. M. Küster. Rule-Based Specification of Behavioral Consistency Based on the UML Meta-model. In Gogolla and Kobryn [GK01], pages 272–286.

[EHKG02]   G. Engels, R. Heckel, J. M. Küster, and L. Groenewegen. Consistency-Preserving Model Evolution through Transformations. In Jézéquel et al. [JHC02], pages 212–226.

[EHKZ05]   C. Ermel, K. Hölscher, S. Kuske, and P. Ziemann. Animated Simulation of Integrated UML Behavioral Models Based on Graph Transformation. In *2005 IEEE Symposium on Visual Languages and Human-Centric Computing (VL/HCC 2005), 21-24 September 2005, Dallas, TX, USA*, pages 125–133. IEEE Computer Society, 2005.

[EKHG01]   G. Engels, J. M. Küster, R. Heckel, and L. Groenewegen. A Methodology for Specifying and Analyzing Consistency of Object-oriented Behavioral Models. In V. Gruhn, editor, *European Software Engineering Conference 2001, Vienna, Austria*, volume 1301 of *Lecture Notes in Computer Science*, pages 186–195, Berlin, Heidelberg, 2001. Springer.

[EKMR99]   H. Ehrig, H.-J. Kreowski, U. Montanari, and G. Rozenberg, editors. *Handbook of Graph Grammars and Computing by Graph Transformation, Vol. 3: Concurrency, Parallelism, and Distribution*, volume 3. World Scientific, Singapore, 1999.

[EM85]   H. Ehrig and B. Mahr. *Fundamentals of Algebraic Specification 1: Equations and Initial Semantics*, volume 6 of *EATCS Monographs in Theoretical Computer Science*. Springer, Berlin, Heidelberg, 1985.

[EPT04]   H. Ehrig, U. Prange, and G. Taentzer. Fundamental theory for typed attributed graph transformation. In H. Ehrig, G. Engels, F. Parisi-Presicce, and Rozenberg G., editors, *Graph Transformations, Proceedings of the 2nd Intl. Conference on Graph*

Transformations (ICGT 2004), volume 3256 of *Lecture Notes in Computer Science*, pages 161–177, Berlin, Heidelberg, 2004. Springer.

[ERT99] C. Ermel, M. Rudolf, and G. Taentzer. The AGG Approach: Language and Environment. In Ehrig et al. [EEKR99], pages 551–603.

[FHS04] M. Freitag, O. Herzog, and B. Scholz-Reiter. Selbststeuerung logistischer Prozesse – Ein Paradigmenwechsel und seine Grenzen. *Industrie Management*, 20(1):23–27, 2004.

[FKZ76] R. Farrow, K. Kennedy, and L. Zucconi. Graph Grammars and Global Program Data Flow Analysis. In *17th Annual Symposium on Foundations of Computer Science, 25-27 October 1976, Houston, Texas, USA*, pages 42–56. IEEE, 1976.

[GADP89] S. Goss, S. Aron, J.-L. Deneubourg, and J.-M. Pasteels. Self-Organized Shortcuts in the Argentine Ant. *Naturwissenschaften*, 76, 1989.

[GBG⁺06] R. Geiß, G.V. Batz, D. Grund, S. Hack, and A. Szalkowski. GrGen: A Fast SPO-Based Graph Rewriting Tool. In Corradini et al. [CEM⁺06], pages 383–397.

[GK01] M. Gogolla and C. Kobryn, editors. *UML 2001 - The Unified Modeling Language, Modeling Languages, Concepts, and Tools, 4th International Conference, Toronto, Canada, October 1-5, 2001, Proceedings*, volume 2185 of *Lecture Notes in Computer Science*, Berlin, Heidelberg, 2001. Springer.

[HHS04] J. H. Hausmann, R. Heckel, and S. Sauer. Dynamic Meta Modeling with time: Specifying the semantics of multimedia sequence diagrams. *Software and System Modeling*, 3(3):181–193, 2004.

[HKK06a] K. Hölscher, P. Knirsch, and H.-J. Kreowski. Modelling Transport Networks by Means of Autonomous Units. In H.-D. Haasis, H. Kopfer, and J. Schönberger, editors, *Operations Research Proceedings 2005*, pages 399–404, Berlin, Heidelberg, 2006. Springer.

[HKK06b]   K. Hölscher, H.-J. Kreowski, and S. Kuske. Autonomous Units and their Semantics — the Sequential Case. In Corradini et al. [CEM+06], pages 245–259.

[HKK+07]   K. Hölscher, R. Klempien-Hinrichs, P. Knirsch, H.-J. Kreowski, and S. Kuske. Autonomous Units: Basic Concepts and Semantic Foundation. In M. Hülsmann and K. Windt, editors, *Understanding Autonomous Cooperation and Control in Logistics – The Impact on Management, Information and Communication and Material Flow*, pages 103–120. Springer, Berlin, Heidelberg, 2007.

[HKK08]   K. Hölscher, R. Klempien-Hinrichs, and P. Knirsch. Undecidable Control Conditions in Graph Transformation Units. In A.M. Moreira and L. Ribeiro, editors, *Proceedings of the Brazilian Symposium on Formal Methods (SBMF 2006)*, volume 195 of *Electronic Notes in Theoretical Computer Science*, pages 95–111. Elsevier Science, 2008.

[HKL08]   K. Hölscher, P. Knirsch, and M. Luderer. Autonomous units for communication-based dynamic scheduling. In H.-D. Haasis, H.-J. Kreowski, and B. Scholz-Reiter, editors, *Dynamics in Logistics, Proceedings of the 1st Intl. Conference LDIC 2007*, pages 331–339, Berlin, Heidelberg, 2008. Springer.

[HKT02]   R. Heckel, J. Küster, and G. Taentzer. Confluence of typed attributed graph transformation systems. In Corradini et al. [CEKR02], pages 161–176.

[HM00]   B. Hoffmann and M. Minas. A Generic Model for Diagram Syntax and Semantics. In Rolim et al. [RBC+00], pages 443–450.

[HMU01]   J. E. Hopcroft, R. Motwani, and J. D. Ullman. *Introduction to Automata Theory, Languages, and Computation*. Addison Wesley, Reading, Massachusetts, USA, 2001.

[HP01]   A. Habel and D. Plump. Computational Completeness of Programming Languages based on Graph Transformation. In F. Honsell and M. Miculan, editors, *Proc. FoSSaCS 2001*, volume 2030 of *Lecture Notes in Computer Science*, pages 230–245, Berlin, Heidelberg, 2001. Springer.

[HZ01]   R. Heckel and A. Zündorf. How to Specify a Graph Transformation Approach - A Meta Model for Fujaba. In H. Ehrig and J. Padberg, editors, *Uniform Approaches to Graphical Process Specification Techniques, Satellite Workshop of ETAPS 2001, Genova, Italy*, volume 44.4 of *Electronic Notes in Theoretical Computer Science*, pages 41–51. Elsevier Science, 2001.

[HZG06]   K. Hölscher, P. Ziemann, and M. Gogolla. On Translating UML Models into Graph Transformation Systems. *Journal of Visual Languages and Computing*, 17(1):78–105, 2006.

[JHC02]   J.-M. Jézéquel, H. Hußmann, and S. Cook, editors. *UML 2002 - The Unified Modeling Language, 5th International Conference, Dresden, Germany, September 30 - October 4, 2002, Proceedings*, volume 2460 of *Lecture Notes in Computer Science*, Berlin, Heidelberg, 2002. Springer.

[KE01]   J. Kennedy and R. C. Eberhart. *Swarm Intelligence*. Morgan Kaufmann Publishers, San Fransisco, USA, 2001.

[KGKK02]   S. Kuske, M. Gogolla, R. Kollmann, and H.-J. Kreowski. An Integrated Semantics for UML Class, Object and State Diagrams Based on Graph Transformation. In M. J. Butler, L. Petre, and K. Sere, editors, *Integrated Formal Methods, Third International Conference, IFM 2002, Turku, Finland, May 15-18, 2002, Proceedings*, volume 2335 of *Lecture Notes in Computer Science*, pages 11–28, Berlin, Heidelberg, 2002. Springer.

[KHK06]   H.-J. Kreowski, K. Hölscher, and P. Knirsch. Semantics of Visual Models in a Rule-based Setting. In R. Heckel, editor, *Proceedings of the School of SegraVis Research Training Network on Foundations of Visual Modelling Techniques (FoVMT 2004), Dagstuhl*, volume 148 of *Electronic Notes in Theoretical Computer Science*, pages 75–88. Elsevier Science, 2006.

[KK99a]   H.-J. Kreowski and S. Kuske. Graph Transformation Units and Modules. In Ehrig et al. [EEKR99], pages 607–638.

[KK99b]   H.-J. Kreowski and S. Kuske. Graph transformation units with interleaving semantics. *Formal Aspects of Computing*, 11(6):690–723, 1999.

[KK07]   H.-J. Kreowski and S. Kuske. Autonomous units and their se-
           mantics - the parallel case. In J.L. Fiadeiro and P.Y. Schobbens,
           editors, *Recent Trends in Algebraic Development Techniques,
           18th International Workshop, WADT 2006*, volume 4409 of
           Lecture Notes in Computer Science, pages 56–73, Berlin, Hei-
           delberg, 2007. Springer.

[KKK02]   R. Klempien-Hinrichs, P. Knirsch, and S. Kuske. Modeling
           the pickup-and-delivery problem with structured graph trans-
           formation. In H.-J. Kreowski and P. Knirsch, editors, *Proc.
           Applied Graph Transformation (AGT'02)*, 2002. 119–130.

[KKS97]   H.-J. Kreowski, S. Kuske, and A. Schürr. Nested Graph Trans-
           formation Units. *International Journal on Software Engineer-
           ing and Knowledge Engineering*, 7(4):479–502, 1997.

[KMA82]   A. J. Kfoury, R. N. Moll, and M. A. Arbib. *A Programming
           Approach to Computability*. Springer, Berlin, Heidelberg, 1982.

[Kre78]   H.-J. Kreowski. *Manipulationen von Graphmanipulationen*.
           PhD thesis, Universität Berlin, 1978.

[Kre93]   H.-J. Kreowski. Translations into the Graph Grammar Ma-
           chine. In R. M. Sleep, R. Plasmeijer, and M. van Eekelen, edi-
           tors, *Term Graph Rewriting: Theory and Practice*, chapter 13,
           pages 171–183. John Wiley, 1993.

[Kuh02]   A. Kuhn. Prozessketten – ein Modell für die Logistik. In H.-P.
           Wiendahl, editor, *Erfolgsfaktor Logistikqualität*, pages 58–72.
           Springer, Berlin, Heidelberg, 2002.

[Kus00a]   S. Kuske. More About Control Conditions for Transformation
           Units. In H. Ehrig, G. Engels, H.-J. Kreowski, and G. Rozen-
           berg, editors, *Theory and Application of Graph Transforma-
           tions*, volume 1764 of *Lecture Notes in Computer Science*, pages
           323–337, Berlin, Heidelberg, 2000. Springer.

[Kus00b]   S. Kuske. *Transformation Units—A structuring Principle for
           Graph Transformation Systems*. PhD thesis, Universität Bre-
           men, 2000.

[Kus01]   S. Kuske. A Formal Semantics of UML State Machines Based
           on Structured Graph Transformation. In Gogolla and Kobryn
           [GK01], pages 241–256.

[LK73]   S. Lin and B. W. Kernighan. An effective heuristic algo-
            rithm for the traveling salesman problem. *Operations Research*,
            21(9):498–516, 1973.

[Mes92]   J. Meseguer. Conditioned Rewriting Logic as a United Model
            of Concurrency. *Theoretical Computer Science*, 96(1):73–155,
            1992.

[MSP94]   A. Maggiolo-Schettini and A. Peron. Semantics of Full Stat-
            echarts Based on Graph Rewriting. In H. J. Schneider
            and H. Ehrig, editors, *Graph Transformations in Computer
            Science, International Workshop, Dagstuhl Castle, Germany,
            January 1993, Proceedings*, volume 776 of *Lecture Notes in
            Computer Science*, pages 265–279, Berlin, Heidelberg, 1994.
            Springer.

[Plu98]   D. Plump. Termination of graph rewriting is undecidable. *Fun-
            damenta Informaticae*, 33(2):201–209, 1998.

[Pra71]   T. W. Pratt. Pair Grammars, Graph Languages and String-to-
            Graph Translations. *Journal of Computer and System Science*,
            5(6):560–595, 1971.

[PRS98]   G. Păun, G. Rozenberg, and A. Salomaa. *DNA Computing —
            New Computing Paradigms*. Springer, Berlin, Heidelberg, 1998.

[RBC+00]   J.D.P. Rolim, A.Z. Broder, A. Corradini, R. Gorrieri,
            R. Heckel, J. Hromkovic, U. Vaccaro, and J.B. Wells, editors.
            Proc. ICALP Workshops 2000, Proceedings in Informatics 8.
            Carleton Scientific, 2000.

[Rei98]   W. Reisig. *Elements of Distributed Algorithms – Modeling and
            Analysis with Petri Nets*. Springer, Berlin, Heidelberg, 1998.

[Roz97]   G. Rozenberg, editor. *Handbook of Graph Grammars and Com-
            puting by Graph Transformations, Volume 1: Foundations*, vol-
            ume 1. World Scientific, Singapore, 1997.

[RS97]   G. Rozenberg and A. Salomaa, editors. *Handbook of Formal
            Languages, Vol. 1–3*. Springer, Berlin, Heidelberg, 1997.

[Sch95]   A. Schürr. Specification of Graph Translators with Triple
            Graph Grammars. In E. W. Mayr, G. Schmidt, and G. Tin-
            hofer, editors, *Graph-Theoretic Concepts in Computer Science*,

20th International Workshop, WG '94, Herrsching, Germany, June 16-18, 1994, Proceedings, volume 903 of *Lecture Notes in Computer Science*, pages 151–163, Berlin, Heidelberg, 1995. Springer.

[Sch02]   A.-W. Scheer. *Vom Geschäftsprozeß zum Anwendungssystem.* Springer, Berlin, Heidelberg, 2002.

[SS95]   M. W. P. Savelsbergh and M. Sol. The general pickup and delivery problem. *Transportation Science*, 29(1):17–29, 1995.

[SWZ99]   A. Schürr, A. Winter, and A. Zündorf. PROGRES: Language and Environment. In Ehrig et al. [EEKR99], pages 487–550.

[TE00]   A. Tsiolakis and H. Ehrig. Consistency Analysis of UML Class and Sequence Diagrams using Attributed Graph Grammars. In H. Ehrig and G. Taentzer, editors, *Proc. of Joint APPLIGRAPH/GETGRATS Workshop on Graph Transformation Systems, Berlin, March 2000*, pages 77–86, 2000.

[Var02]   D. Varró. A Formal Semantics of UML Statecharts by Model Transition Systems. In Corradini et al. [CEKR02], pages 378–392.

[Wei99]   G. Weiss, editor. *Multiagent Systems - A Modern Approach to Distributed Artificial Intelligence.* The MIT Press, 1999.

[Wol02]   S. Wolfram. *A New Kind of Science.* Wolfram Media, 2002.

[ZHG05a]   P. Ziemann, K. Hölscher, and M. Gogolla. Coherently Explaining UML Statechart and Collaboration Diagrams by Graph Transformations. In A. Mota and A. Moura, editors, *Proceedings of the Brazilian Symposium on Formal Methods (SBMF 2004)*, volume 130 of *Electronic Notes in Theoretical Computer Science*, pages 263–280. Elsevier Science, 2005.

[ZHG05b]   P. Ziemann, K. Hölscher, and M. Gogolla. From UML Models to Graph Transformation Systems. In M. Minas, editor, *Proceedings of the Workshop on Visual Languages and Formal Methods (VLFM 2004)*, volume 127(4) of *Electronic Notes in Theoretical Computer Science*, pages 17–33. Elsevier Science, 2005.